# שירים וזמירות
# SONGS AND HYMNS

### A Musical Supplement To
# Gates of Prayer
# שערי תפלה

# שירים וזמירות
# SONGS AND HYMNS

A Musical Supplement To

## Gates of Prayer

שערי תפלה

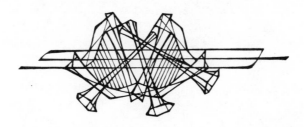

published by
AMERICAN CONFERENCE OF CANTORS
and
CENTRAL CONFERENCE OF AMERICAN RABBIS

with drawings by Ismar David

JOINT PUBLICATION COMMITTEE
OF THE
AMERICAN CONFERENCE OF CANTORS
AND THE
CENTRAL CONFERENCE OF AMERICAN RABBIS

*Co-Chairmen:*

Cantor Raymond Smolover    Rabbi Malcolm Stern

*Committee*

CANTOR NORMAN BELINK         RABBI CHARLES ANNES

CANTOR RAMON GILBERT         RABBI BERNARD SCHACHTEL

CANTOR STEPHEN RICHARDS      RABBI CHAIM STERN

*Editorial Board*

DR. JACK GOTTLIEB

CANTOR RAYMOND SMOLOVER AND RABBI MALCOLM STERN

# Contents

INTRODUCTION  ix

A WORD ABOUT USAGE  xi

CONTENTS

# Introduction

שירים וזמירות SONGS AND HYMNS was born out of the need to provide melodies for the song-texts listed on pages 726 and 727 of שערי תפלה GATES OF PRAYER.

These songs come from such a variety of sources that the Committee found it advisable to make them readily available. The Joint Publication Committee of the Central Conference of American Rabbis and of the American Conference of Cantors was charged with the task of compiling this book, and they found the search for appropriate melodies a difficult and time-consuming one. Therefore, recognizing the urgent need for the song supplement to GATES OF PRAYER, this task was undertaken first.

A larger work, שערי שירה GATES OF SONG, is in preparation. It will contain musical settings for other portions of the liturgy.

The following guidelines have been followed in producing this work:

1. Every listed song is provided with a melody, usually one in current use.

2. Transliterations follow precisely those in GATES OF PRAYER even though this has necessitated some adjustments in notation, especially whenever a vocal *sheva* occurs.

3. Chordings have been made as simple as possible with due regard for variety and avoidance of the commonplace. In a few places more sophisticated chording has been printed in parentheses. The chords are designed for keyboard or guitar accompaniment.

4. Wherever possible texts and melodies have been traced to their original sources and these sources are indicated.

5. Tempo markings are given by metronomic numbering, and the character of each song is described by an adverb, rather than employing the traditional Italian phraseology.

6. Indications of loudness and softness have not been provided since dynamics will be governed by place of performance and nature of use.

The Joint Publication Committee owes a special debt of gratitude to Jack Gottlieb, Professor of Music at the School of Sacred Music, Hebrew Union College - Jewish Institute of Religion, for giving so generously of his expertise and for his dedicated labors in all phases of this project.

We are grateful, also, to Mr. Richard Neumann, Music Director of the New York Board of Jewish Education; to the late Cantor Arthur Wolfson, and to composers Charles Davidson, Michael Isaacson, and Ben Steinberg, who were helpful in the planning stages of this work. The first version of the guitar chording was provided by David Stern and David Smolover, guitarists. Cantor Albert Sturmer made a most generous contribution.

The project was initiated by Rabbi Joseph Glaser, Executive Vice-President of the Central Conference of American Rabbis; and Rabbi A. Stanley Dreyfus, Chairman of the Committee on Liturgy of the Central Conference of American Rabbis, lent his scholarly counsel, as did Rabbi Chaim Stern, Editor of GATES OF PRAYER. Rabbi Leonard Schoolman and Mr. Ralph Davis of the Union of American Hebrew Congregations have helped immeasurably in bringing this volume to publication.

To all the above, as well as to the members of the Joint Publication Committee, we express our sincerest appreciation for their cooperation and efforts.

CANTOR RAYMOND SMOLOVER   RABBI MALCOLM STERN

*Co-Chairmen*

# A Word About Usage

שירים וזמירות, Songs and Hymns, is designed for maximum participation in worship by congregations, religious schools, youth groups, camps — wherever Jews pray and sing. Some of the melodies may be familiar to some groups, totally unknown to others. The Committee has selected those melodies which adhere most closely to the texts published in GATES OF PRAYER.

We urge you, the user, to experiment with the widest variety of songs and hymns that your circumstances permit. The Editorial Board would appreciate learning from you which songs, in your opinion, merit preservation for our future volume, GATES OF SONG.

# A NOTE ON TRANSLITERATION

The system employed in this Prayerbook is, with minor deviations, the "Proposed Standard Romanization of Hebrew" prepared for the American National Standards Institute.

## Vowels and Consonants for Special Notice

*a*   as in 'papa' (short) or 'father' (long)

*e*   as in 'get' or 'the' (sheva)

*eh*  as in 'get' (used only at the end of a word)

*i*   as in 'bit' (short) or 'machine' (long)

*o*   as in 'often'

*u*   as in 'pull' (short) or 'rule' (long)

*ai*  as in 'aisle'

*oi*  as in 'boil'

*ei*  as in 'veil'

*g*   as in 'get' (hard 'g')

*ch*  as in Scottish 'loch' or German 'ach'

# שירים וזמירות

# SONGS AND HYMNS

# ADON OLAM

Piyyut

Eliezer Gerovitch

He is the eternal Lord, who reigned before any being had yet been created; when all was done according to His will, already then His name was King.

And after all has ceased to be, still will He reign in solitary majesty; He was, He is, and He shall be in glory.

And He is One; none other can compare to Him, or consort with Him; He is without beginning, without end; to Him belong power and dominion.

And He is *my* God, my living Redeemer, my Rock in time of trouble and distress; He is my banner and my refuge, my benefactor when I call on Him.

Into His hands I entrust my spirit, when I sleep and when I wake; and with my spirit, my body also: the Lord is with me, I will not fear.

2

A·don o·lam, a·sher ma·lach
  be·te·rem kol ye·tsir niv·ra,
le·eit na·a·sa ve·chef·tso kol,
  a·zai me·lech she·mo nik·ra.
Ve·a·cha·rei ki·che·lot ha·kol,
  le·va·do yim·loch no·ra,
ve·hu ha·ya, ve·hu ho·veh,
  ve·hu yi·he·yeh be·tif·a·ra.
Ve·hu e·chad, ve·ein shei·ni
  le·ham·shil lo, le·hach·bi·ra,

be·li rei·shit, be·li tach·lit,
  ve·lo ha·oz ve·ha·mis·ra.
Ve·hu Ei·li, ve·chai go·a·li,
  ve·tsur chev·li be·eit tsa·ra,
ve·hu ni·si u·ma·nos li,
  me·nat ko·si be·yom ek·ra.
Be·ya·do af·kid ru·chi
  be·eit i·shan ve·a·i·ra,
ve·im ru·chi ge·vi·ya·ti:
  A·do·nai li, ve·lo i·ra.

When this, our world, shall be no more,
In majesty He still shall reign,
Who was, who is, who will remain,
His endless glory we proclaim.

Alone is He, beyond compare,
Without division or ally,
Without initial date or end,
Omnipotent He rules on high.

He is my God, my Savior He,
To whom I turn in sorrow's hour —
My banner proud, my refuge sure,
Who hears and answers with His pow'r.

Then in His hand myself I lay,
And trusting sleep, and wake with cheer;
My soul and body are His care;
The Lord does guard, I have no fear.

# AL HANISIM

Talmud: *Soferim* 20:8

Folk Melody

**Resolutely ( ♩ = 69)**

Refrain:
Al ha - ni - sim ve - al ha - pur - kan, ve -
al ha - ge - vu - rot, ve - al ha - te - shu - ot, ve -
al ha - mil - cha - mot, she - a - si - ta la - a - vo - tei - nu,
ba - ya - mim ha - heim, ba - ze - man ha - zeh, ba - ze - man ha -
zeh. 1. Bi - mei ___ Ma - tit - ya - hu, Ma - tit - ya - hu ben Yo -
cha - nan ko - hein ___ ga - dol Chash - mo -
na - i u - va - nav, ke - she - am - e - da mal -
chut ___ Ya - van al a - me - cha Yis - ra - eil, al

| | |
|---|---|
| Al ha·ni·sim ve·al ha·pur·kan, | עַל הַנִּסִּים, וְעַל הַפֻּרְקָן, |
| ve·al ha·ge·vu·rot, ve·al ha·te·shu·ot, | וְעַל הַגְּבוּרוֹת, וְעַל הַתְּשׁוּעוֹת, |
| ve·al ha·mil·cha·mot, | וְעַל הַמִּלְחָמוֹת, |
| she·a·si·ta la·a·vo·tei·nu, | שֶׁעָשִׂיתָ לַאֲבוֹתֵינוּ |
| ba·ya·mim ha·heim, ba·ze·man ha·zeh. | בַּיָּמִים הָהֵם, בַּזְּמַן הַזֶּה. |
| Bi·mei Ma·tit·ya·hu ben Yo·cha·nan | בִּימֵי מַתִּתְיָהוּ בֶּן־יוֹחָנָן |
| ko·hein ga·dol Chash·mo·na·i u·va·nav, | כֹּהֵן גָּדוֹל חַשְׁמוֹנַאי וּבָנָיו, |
| ke·she·a·me·da mal·chut Ya·van | כְּשֶׁעָמְדָה מַלְכוּת יָוָן |
| al a·me·cha Yis·ra·eil, | עַל עַמְּךָ יִשְׂרָאֵל, |
| le·hash·ki·cham To·ra·te·cha, | לְהַשְׁכִּיחָם תּוֹרָתֶךָ, |
| u·le·ha·a·vi·ram mei·chu·kei re·tso·ne·cha. | וּלְהַעֲבִירָם מֵחֻקֵּי רְצוֹנֶךָ. |
| Ve·a·ta be·ra·cha·me·cha ha·ra·bim, | וְאַתָּה בְּרַחֲמֶיךָ הָרַבִּים, |
| a·mad·ta la·hem be·eit tsa·ra·tam. | עָמַדְתָּ לָהֶם בְּעֵת צָרָתָם. |

*The translation of Al Hanisim is on page 45.*

# AL SHELOSHA DEVARIM

*Pirkei Avot* 1:2                                                        Chaim Zur

| Al she·lo·sha de·va·rim | עַל־שְׁלשָׁה דְבָרִים |
| ha·o·lam o·meid: | הָעוֹלָם עוֹמֵד: |
| al ha·torah, | עַל הַתּוֹרָה, |
| ve·al ha·a·vo·da, | וְעַל הָעֲבוֹדָה, |
| ve·al ge·mi·lut cha·sa·dim. | וְעַל גְּמִילוּת חֲסָדִים. |

The world depends on three things: on Torah, on worship, and on loving deeds.

(p. 710)

# ALL THE WORLD

Israel Zangwill

A. W. Binder

**Majestically ( ♩ = 100)**

All the world shall come to serve You, and__ bless Your glo-rious name, And Your right-eous-ness tri-um-phant the__ is-lands shall pro-claim. And the peo-ples__ shall go seek-ing who knew____ You not be-fore, And the ends of earth shall praise You, and__ tell__ Your great-ness o'er.

All the world shall come to serve You,
    And bless Your glorious name,
And Your righteousness triumphant
    The islands shall proclaim.
And the peoples shall go seeking
    Who knew You not before,
And the ends of earth shall praise You,
    And tell Your greatness o'er.

They shall build for You their altars,
    Their idols overthrown,
And their graven gods shall shame them,
    As they turn to You alone.

They shall worship You at sunrise,
    And feel Your kingdom's might,
And impart their understanding
    To those astray in night.

With the coming of Your kingdom
    The hills shall shout with song,
And the islands laugh exultant
    That they to God belong.
And through all Your congregations
    So loud Your praise shall ring,
That the utmost peoples, hearing,
    Shall hail You crowned King.

7

# (40)
# AMAR RABBI AKIVA

Sifra: *Kedoshim*                                      Folk Melody

A·mar Ra·bi A·ki·va [3]

Ve·a·hav·ta le·rei·a·cha ka·mo·cha:

zeh ke·lal ga·dol ba·to·rah.

אָמַר רַבִּי עֲקִיבָא

וְאָהַבְתָּ לְרֵעֲךָ כָּמוֹךָ:

זֶה כְּלָל גָּדוֹל בַּתּוֹרָה.

Said Rabbi Akiva: "You shall love your neighbor as yourself" — this is the great principle of the Torah.

# AMAR RABBI ELAZAR

Talmud: *Berakot* 64 A

Folk Melody

A·mar Ra·bi El·a·zar,
a·mar Ra·bi Cha·ni·na:
Tal·mi·dei cha·cha·mim
mar·bim sha·lom ba·o·lam.

אָמַר רַבִּי אֶלְעָזָר,
אָמַר רַבִּי חֲנִינָא:
תַּלְמִידֵי חֲכָמִים
מַרְבִּים שָׁלוֹם בָּעוֹלָם.

Rabbi Elazar said, quoting Rabbi Chanina: "The disciples of the wise (students of Torah) add peace to the world."

# AMERICA THE BEAUTIFUL

Katherine Lee Bates

Samuel Augustus Ward

O beau - ti-ful for spa - cious skies, for am - ber waves of grain, For pur - ple moun - tain maj - es - ties a - bove the fruit - ed plain! A - mer - i - ca! A - mer - i - ca! God shed His grace on thee, and crown thy good with broth - er-hood from sea to shin - ing sea.

O beautiful for pilgrim feet,
Whose stern, impassioned stress,
A thoroughfare for freedom beat,
Across the wilderness!
America! America!
God mend thy every flaw,
Confirm thy soul in self-control,
Thy liberty in law!

O beautiful for heroes proved
In liberating strife,
Who more than self their country loved,
And mercy more than life!

America! America!
May God thy gold refine
Til all success be nobleness,
And ev'ry gain divine!

O beautiful for patriot dream,
That sees beyond the years,
Thine alabaster cities gleam,
Undimmed by human tears!
America! America!
God shed His grace on thee,
And crown thy good with brotherhood,
From sea to shining sea!

11

(46)
# ANI MAAMIN

Moses Maimonides

Folk Melody

Be - vi - at _____ ha - ma - shi - ach Be -
af al pi she - yit - ma - he - mei - a, im
Im kol zeh _____ a - cha - keh lo be -

vi - at ha - ma - shi - ach a - ni ma - a - min.
kol _____ zeh _____ a _____ ni ma - a - min.
chol _____ yom _____ she - ya - vo. _____

A·ni ma·a·min be·e·mu·na she·lei·ma
be·vi·at ha·ma·shi·ach.
Ve·af al pi she·yit·ma·he·mei·a,
im kol zeh a·ni ma·a·min,
im kol zeh a·cha·keh lo
be·chol yom she·ya·vo.

אֲנִי מַאֲמִין בֶּאֱמוּנָה שְׁלֵמָה
בְּבִיאַת הַמָּשִׁיחַ.
וְאַף עַל פִּי שֶׁיִּתְמַהְמֵהַּ,
עִם כָּל זֶה אֲנִי מַאֲמִין,
עִם כָּל זֶה אֲחַכֶּה לֹו
בְּכָל יֹום שֶׁיָּבוֹא.

I believe with perfect faith
in the Messiah's coming.
And even if he be delayed,
I will await him.

# ANIM ZEMIROT

Ascribed to Judah of Regensburg, 13th C.

Heinrich Schalit

Lyrically ( ♩ = 70)

An-im ze-mi-rot ve-shi-rim e-e-rog,
Ki ei-le-cha naf-shi ta-a-rog. Naf-
shi chi-me-da be-tseil ya-de-cha, la
da-at kol raz so-de-cha.

An·im ze·mi·rot ve·shi·rim e·e·rog,
ki ei·le·cha naf·shi ta·a·rog.
Naf·shi chi·me·da be·tseil ya·de·cha,
la·da·at kol raz so·de·cha.
Mi·dei da·be·ri bi·che·vo·de·cha,
ho·meh li·bi el do·de·cha.
Ye·e·rav na si·chi a·le·cha,
ki naf·shi ta·a·rog ei·le·cha.

אַנְעִים זְמִירוֹת וְשִׁירִים אֶאֱרוֹג,
כִּי אֵלֶיךָ נַפְשִׁי תַעֲרוֹג.
נַפְשִׁי חָמְדָה בְּצֵל יָדֶךָ,
לָדַעַת כָּל־רָז סוֹדֶךָ.
מִדֵּי דַבְּרִי בִּכְבוֹדֶךָ,
הוֹמֶה לִבִּי אֶל־דּוֹדֶיךָ.
יֶעֱרַב־נָא שִׂיחִי עָלֶיךָ,
כִּי נַפְשִׁי תַעֲרוֹג אֵלֶיךָ.

I make pleasant songs, and weave verses, because my soul longs for You. To
know Your deepest secret, to be in Your hand's shade, is my soul's strongest
wish. My heart yearns for Your love, whenever I speak of Your glory. So
may my thought be sweet to You, for whom my soul longs.

# ASHREINU

Liturgy                                                                 Shpirvarg

Ash·rei·nu! Ma tov chel·kei·nu!                     אַשְׁרֵינוּ! מַה־טּוֹב חֶלְקֵנוּ!

U·ma na·im go·ra·lei·nu!                             וּמַה־נָּעִים גּוֹרָלֵנוּ!

U·ma ya·fa ye·ru·sha·tei·nu!                         וּמַה־יָפָה יְרֻשָׁתֵנוּ!

How greatly we are blessed! How good is our portion! How pleasant our
lot! How beautiful our heritage!

(30 & 62)

# ATA ECHAD
# WHEN THIS SONG OF PRAISE

Liturgy
English: William Cullen Bryant

Chassidic Melody

**Liltingly** (♩ = 104)

**Em**    **Em7**      **Am**

A - ta e - chad ve - shim - cha e - chad___ u -
*When this song of praise shall cease___*

**Em**    **C**      **Em**    **A**

mi___ ke - a - me cha_____ Yis - ra - eil, u -
*Let___ Your___ chil - dren,___ Lord, de - part*

**Em7**      **Am**

mi Ke - a - me - cha Yis - ra - eil_____
*With the bless - ing of Your peace,___*

**C**    **D7**      **Em**    *Fine*

Hebrew

goi e - chad___ ba - a - rets?

**C**    **Dm**      **E**

English

*And Your love in ev - ery heart.*

**G**      **D**      **Em7**    **C**

Tif - e - ret_____ ge - du - la

**B7**      **C**      **Am**    **Em**

va - a - te - ret_____ ye - shu - a,

16

yom me-nu-cha u-ke-du-sha___ le-a-me-cha na-ta-ta,

yom me-nu-cha u-ke-du-sha___ la-a-me-cha na-ta-ta.

| | |
|---|---|
| A·ta e·chad ve·shi·me·cha e·chad | אַתָּה אֶחָד וְשִׁמְךָ אֶחָד |
| u·mi ke·a·me·cha Yis·ra·eil, [2] | וּמִי כְּעַמְּךָ יִשְׂרָאֵל, (2) |
| goi e·chad ba·a·rets? | גּוֹי אֶחָד בָּאָרֶץ? |
| Tif·e·ret ge·du·la va·a·te·ret ye·shu·a, | תִּפְאֶרֶת גְּדֻלָּה וַעֲטֶרֶת יְשׁוּעָה, |
| yom me·nu·cha u·ke·du·sha<br>le·a·me·cha na·ta·ta. | יוֹם מְנוּחָה וּקְדֻשָּׁה לְעַמְּךָ נָתָתָ. |
| A·ta e·chad ve·shi·me·cha e·chad | אַתָּה אֶחָד וְשִׁמְךָ אֶחָד |
| u·mi ke·a·me·cha Yis·ra·eil [2] | וּמִי כְּעַמְּךָ יִשְׂרָאֵל, (2) |
| goi e·chad ba·a·rets... | גּוֹי אֶחָד בָּאָרֶץ. |

You are One, Your name is One, and there is none like Your people Israel, a unique people on earth. A garland of glory have You given us, a crown of salvation: a day of rest and holiness. You are One . . . .

### FATHER, HEAR THE PRAYER

Father, hear the prayer we offer,
Not for ease that prayer shall be,
But for strength that we may ever
Live our lives courageously.

Be our strength in hours of weakness,
In our wanderings be our guide;
Through endeavor, failure, danger,
Be for ever at our side.

### WHEN THIS SONG OF PRAISE

When this song of praise shall cease,
Let Your children, Lord, depart,
With the blessing of Your peace,
And Your love in every heart.

Oh, where-e'er our path may lie,
Father, let us not forget,
That we walk beneath Your eye,
That Your care upholds us yet.

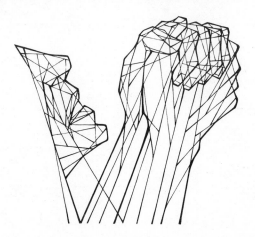

# BARUCH ELOHEINU

Liturgy

Folk Melody

**Resolutely ( ♩ = 104)**

Ba-ruch E - lo-hei - nu she-be-ra - a - nu li-che-vo - do,

Ba-ruch E - lo - hei-nu she-be-ra - a - nu li-che-vo - do,

Ba-ruch E - lo - hei - nu she-be-ra - a - nu li-che-vo - do,

li - che - vo - do, Ve - hiv - di - la - nu

min ha - to - im, ve - na-tan la - nu To - rat e - met ve-

cha - yei o - lam na - ta be - to - chei_____ nu.

| | |
|---|---|
| Ba·ruch E·lo·hei·nu | בָּרוּךְ אֱלֹהֵינוּ |
| she·be·ra·a·nu li·che·vo·do, | שֶׁבְּרָאָנוּ לִכְבוֹדוֹ, |
| ve·hiv·di·la·nu min ha·to·im, | וְהִבְדִּילָנוּ מִן־הַתּוֹעִים, |
| ve·na·tan la·nu To·rat e·met | וְנָתַן לָנוּ תּוֹרַת אֱמֶת |
| [ve·cha·yei o·lam na·ta be·to·chei·nu]. | (וְחַיֵּי עוֹלָם נָטַע בְּתוֹכֵנוּ). |

Blessed is our God, who has touched us with His glory, separated us from
error and given us a Torah of truth [implanting within us eternal life].

# (11)
# COME, O HOLY SABBATH EVENING

Harry H. Mayer

Pinchos Jassinowsky
(based on *Shir Hashirim* mode)

Come, O holy Sabbath evening,
Crown our toil with well earned rest;
Bring us hallowed hours of gladness,
Day of days beloved and blest.

Weave your mystic spell around us
With the glow of Sabbath light:

As we read the ancient wisdom,
Learn its laws of truth and right.

Come, O holy Sabbath spirit,
Radiant shine from every eye;
Lending us your benediction,
Filling every heart with joy.

19

# COME, O SABBATH DAY

Gustav Gottheil (and others)                                    A. W. Binder

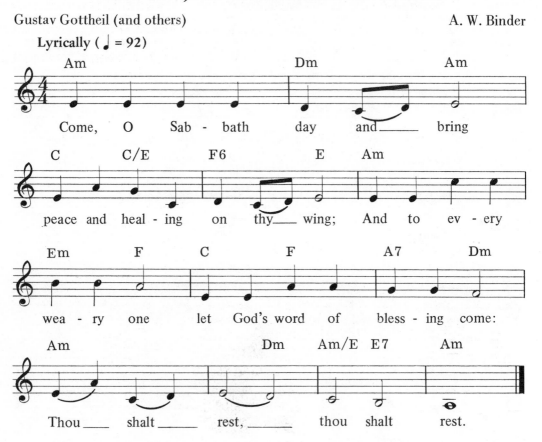

Lyrically ( ♩ = 92)

Am                                        Dm                    Am

Come,   O   Sab - bath   day   and_____   bring

C          C/E          F6                E          Am

peace  and  heal - ing   on   thy___ wing;   And   to   ev - ery

Em            F          C              F          A7            Dm

wea - ry   one     let   God's word   of   bless - ing  come:

Am                            Dm      Am/E  E7        Am

Thou ___ shalt _____ rest, _____ thou  shalt     rest.

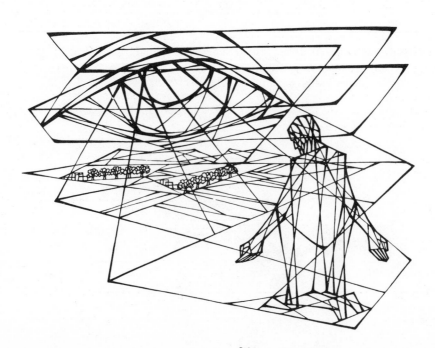

Come, O Sabbath day and bring
Peace and healing on thy wing;
And to every weary one
Let God's word of blessing come:
Thou shalt rest, Thou shalt rest.

Welcome Sabbath, let depart
Every care of troubled heart;
Now the daily task is done,

Let God's word of comfort come:
Thou shalt rest, Thou shalt rest.

Wipe from ev'ry cheek the tear,
Banish care and silence fear;
All things working for the best,
Teach us the divine behest:
Thou shalt rest, Thou shalt rest.

# COULD WE WITH INK

Israel Zangwill

Traditional Melody
(based on *Akdamut* mode)

Tenderly ( ♩ = 88)

21

# (39)
# DAVID MELECH

Liturgy

Mordecai Zeira

David me·lech Yis·ra·eil
chai ve·ka·yam.

דָּוִד מֶלֶךְ יִשְׂרָאֵל
חַי וְקַיָם.

David, king of Israel, lives and endures.

# (21)
# DEROR YIKRA

Ascribed to Dunash b. Labrat, 10th C.

Yemenite Melody

vi ve-u-la-mi ve-ot ye-sha____ a-sei i-
mi. Ne-ta so-rek be-toch car-mi, she-ei shav-
at____ be-nei a-mi. E-lo-him tein ba-mid-bar
har ha-das, shi-ta,____ be-rosh,_ tid-har. Ve-la-maz-
hir ve-la-niz-har she-lo-mim tein____ ke-mei na-har.

| | |
|---|---|
| De·ror yik·ra le·vein im bat, | דְּרוֹר יִקְרָא לְבֵן עִם בַּת, |
| ve·yin·tso·re·chem ke·mo va·vat. | וְיִנְצָרְכֶם כְּמוֹ בָבַת. |
| Ne·im shi·me·chem ve·lo yush·bat, | נְעִים שִׁמְכֶם וְלֹא יֻשְׁבַּת, |
| she·vu ve·nu·chu be·yom Sha·bat. | שְׁבוּ וְנוּחוּ בְּיוֹם שַׁבָּת. |
| De·rosh na·vi ve·u·la·mi | דְּרֹשׁ נָוִי וְאוּלְמִי |
| ve·ot ye·sha a·sei i·mi. | וְאוֹת יֶשַׁע עֲשֵׂה עִמִּי. |
| Ne·ta so·rek be·toch car·mi, | נְטַע שׂוֹרֵק בְּתוֹךְ כַּרְמִי |
| she·ei shav·at be·nei a·mi. | שְׁעֵה שַׁוְעַת בְּנֵי עַמִּי. |
| E·lo·him tein ba·mid·bar har | אֱלֹהִים תֵּן בַּמִּדְבָּר הָר |
| ha·das, shi·ta, be·rosh, tid·har. | הֲדַס, שִׁטָּה, בְּרוֹשׁ, תִּדְהָר. |
| Ve·la·maz·hir ve·la·niz·har | וְלַמַּזְהִיר וְלַנִּזְהָר |
| she·lo·mim tein ke·mei na·har. | שְׁלוֹמִים תֵּן כְּמֵי נָהָר. |

May He proclaim freedom for all His sons and daughters, and keep you as the apple of His eye. Pleasant is your name; it will not be destroyed. Repose, relax, on the Sabbath day. Revisit my holy temple. Give me a sign of deliverance. Plant a vine in my vineyard. Look to my people, hear their laments. Place, O God, in the mountain waste, fir and acacia, myrtle and elm. Give those who teach, and those who obey, abundant peace, like the flow of a stream.

23

(p. 332)

# EARLY WILL I SEEK YOU

Gustav Gottheil (after Solomon ibn Gabirol)

Max Helfman

Lyrically ( ♩ = 80)

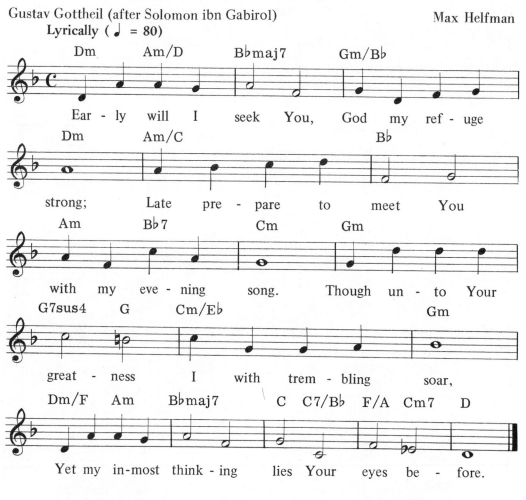

Early will I seek You,
God my refuge strong;
Late prepare to meet You
With my evening song.

Though unto Your greatness
I with trembling soar,
Yet my inmost thinking
Lies Your eyes before.

What this frail heart's dreaming,
And my tongue's poor speech,
Can they even distant
To Your greatness reach?

Being great in mercy,
You will not despise
Praises which till death's hour
From my soul will rise.

שַׁחַר אֲבַקֶּשְׁךָ, צוּרִי וּמִשְׂגַּבִּי,
אֶעֱרוֹךְ לְפָנֶיךָ שַׁחֲרִי וְגַם עַרְבִּי.

לִפְנֵי גְדֻלָּתְךָ אֶעֱמֹד וְאֶבָּהֵל,
כִּי עֵינְךָ תִרְאֶה כָּל מַחְשְׁבוֹת לִבִּי.

מַה-זֶּה אֲשֶׁר יוּכַל הַלֵּב וְהַלָּשׁוֹן
לַעֲשׂוֹת, וּמַה כֹּחַ רוּחִי בְּתוֹךְ קִרְבִּי?

הִנֵּה לְךָ תִיטַב זִמְרַת אֱנוֹשׁ; עַל כֵּן
אוֹדְךָ בְּעוֹד תִּהְיֶה נִשְׁמַת אֱלוֹהַּ בִּי.

# EILEH CHAMEDA LIBI

Piyyut

Chassidic Melody

Ei-leh cha·me·da li·bi

chu·sa na ve·al na tit·a·leim.

אֵלֶּה חָמְדָה לִבִּי

חוּסָה נָא וְאַל נָא תִּתְעַלֵּם.

This is my heart's desire: have pity, do not hide Yourself!

(p. 267)

# EILI, EILI
## (Halichah L'keysariah)

Hannah Senesh    David Zahavi

O Lord, my God,

אֵלִי, אֵלִי,

Ei·li, Ei·li,

I pray that these things never end:

שֶׁלֹּא יִגָּמֵר לְעוֹלָם

she·lo yi·ga·meir le·ol·am

The sand and the sea,

הַחוֹל וְהַיָּם,

ha·chol ve·ha·yam,

The rush of the waters,

רִשְׁרוּשׁ שֶׁל הַמַּיִם,

rish·rush shel ha·ma·yim,

The crash of the heavens,

בְּרַק הַשָּׁמַיִם,

be·rak ha·sha·ma·yim,

The prayer of the heart.

תְּפִלַּת הָאָדָם.

te·fi·lat ha·a·dam.

The sand and the sea,

הַחוֹל וְהַיָּם,

ha·chol ve·ha·yam,

The rush of the waters,

רִשְׁרוּשׁ שֶׁל הַמַּיִם,

rish·rush shel ha·ma·yim,

The crash of the heavens,

בְּרַק הַשָּׁמַיִם,

be·rak ha·sha·ma·yim,

The prayer of the heart.

תְּפִלַּת הָאָדָם.

te·fi·lat ha·a·dam.

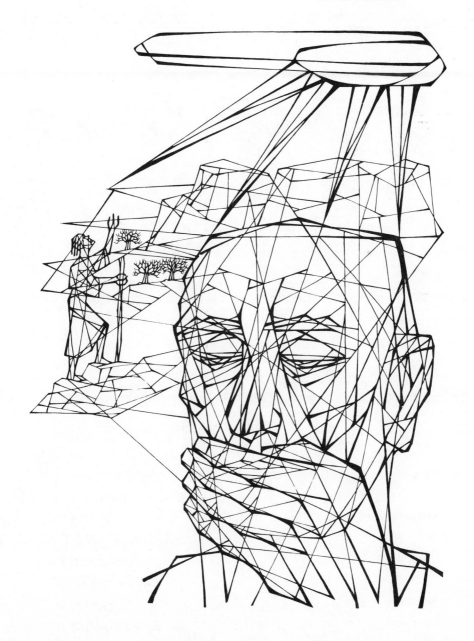

27

# (53)
# EIN ADIR

Piyyut

Sephardic Melody

Ein a·dir ka·a·do·nai
ve·ein ba·ruch ke·ven Am·ram.
Ein ge·do·lah ka·to·rah
ve·ein dar·sha·ne·ha ke·yis·ra·eil.

Mi·pi Eil u·mi·pi Eil
ye·vo·rach kol Yis·ra·eil.

אֵין אַדִּיר כַּיְיָ
וְאֵין בָּרוּךְ כְּבֶן עַמְרָם.
אֵין גְּדוֹלָה כַּתּוֹרָה
וְאֵין דַּרְשָׁנֶיהָ כְּיִשְׂרָאֵל.

מִפִּי אֵל וּמִפִּי אֵל
יְבָרֵךְ כָּל יִשְׂרָאֵל.

| | |
|---|---|
| Ein ha·dur ka·a·do·nai | אֵין הָדוּר כַּיְיָ |
| ve·ein va·tik ke·ven Am·ram. | וְאֵין וָתִיק כְּבֶן עַמְרָם. |
| Ein za·ka ka·to·rah | אֵין זַכָּה כַּתּוֹרָה |
| ve·ein cha·cha·me·ha ke·yis·ra·eil. | וְאֵין חֲכָמֶיהָ כְּיִשְׂרָאֵל. |
| Mi·pi Eil . . . . | מִפִּי אֵל . . . |

| | |
|---|---|
| Ein ta·hor ka·a·do·nai | אֵין טָהוֹר כַּיְיָ |
| ve·ein ya·chid ke·ven Am·ram. | וְאֵין יָחִיד כְּבֶן עַמְרָם. |
| Ein ka·bi·ra ka·to·rah | אֵין כַּבִּירָה כַּתּוֹרָה |
| ve·ein lam·da·ne·ha ke·yis·ra·eil. | וְאֵין לַמְדָנֶיהָ כְּיִשְׂרָאֵל. |
| Mi·pi Eil . . . . | מִפִּי אֵל . . . |

| | |
|---|---|
| Ein po·deh ka·a·do·nai | אֵין פּוֹדֶה כַּיְיָ |
| ve·ein tsa·dik ke·ven Am·ram. | וְאֵין צַדִּיק כְּבֶן עַמְרָם. |
| ein ke·do·sha ka·to·rah | אֵין קְדוֹשָׁה כַּתּוֹרָה |
| ve·ein to·me·che·ha ke·yis·ra·eil. | וְאֵין תּוֹמְכֶיהָ כְּיִשְׂרָאֵל. |
| Mi·pi Eil . . . . | מִפִּי אֵל . . . |

None is mighty as the Lord; none so blessed as Amram's son; nothing is as great as the Torah; none can interpret it as Israel can. *From the mouth of God, the mouth of God, let all Israel be blessed.*

None is glorious as the Lord; none so pious as Amram's son; nothing is as pure as the Torah; none so wise as Israel. *From the mouth . . . .*

None is pure as the Lord; none can match Amram's son; nothing is as mighty as the Torah; none so learned as Israel. *From the mouth . . . .*

None can redeem like the Lord; none is as righteous as Amram's son; nothing is as holy as the Torah; none who hold fast to it as Israel. *From the mouth . . . .*

## (3)

# EIN KEILOHEINU

Medieval text

Julius Freudenthal

Majestically ( ♩ = 104)

1. Ein kei - lo - hei - nu, ein ka - do - nei - nu,

ein ke - mal - kei - nu, ein ___ ke - mo - shi - ei - nu. *Fine*

2. Mi chei - lo - hei - nu? mi cha - do - nei - nu?

*D. C. (al Fine 5th verse)*

mi che - mal - kei - nu? mi ___ che - mo - shi - ei - nu?

| | |
|---|---|
| Ein kei·lo·hei·nu, ein ka·do·nei·nu, | אֵין כֵּאלֹהֵינוּ, אֵין כַּאדוֹנֵינוּ, |
| ein ke·mal·kei·nu, ein ke·mo·shi·ei·nu. | אֵין כְּמַלְכֵּנוּ, אֵין כְּמוֹשִׁיעֵנוּ. |
| Mi chei·lo·hei·nu? Mi cha·do·nei·nu? | מִי כֵאלֹהֵינוּ? מִי כַאדוֹנֵינוּ? |
| Mi che·mal·kei·nu? Mi che·mo·shi·ei·nu? | מִי כְמַלְכֵּנוּ? מִי כְמוֹשִׁיעֵנוּ? |
| No·deh lei·lo·hei·nu, no·deh la·do·nei·nu, | נוֹדֶה לֵאלֹהֵינוּ, נוֹדֶה לַאדוֹנֵינוּ, |
| no·deh le·mal·kei·nu, no·deh le·mo·shi·ei·nu. | נוֹדֶה לְמַלְכֵּנוּ, נוֹדֶה לִמְוֹשִׁיעֵנוּ. |
| Ba·ruch E·lo·hei·nu, ba·ruch A·do·nei·nu, | בָּרוּךְ אֱלֹהֵינוּ, בָּרוּךְ אֲדוֹנֵינוּ, |
| ba·ruch Mal·kei·nu, ba·ruch Mo·shi·ei·nu. | בָּרוּךְ מַלְכֵּנוּ, בָּרוּךְ מוֹשִׁיעֵנוּ. |
| A·ta hu E·lo·hei·nu, | אַתָּה הוּא אֱלֹהֵינוּ, |
| a·ta hu A·do·nei·nu, | אַתָּה הוּא אֲדוֹנֵינוּ, |
| A·ta hu Mal·kei·nu, | אַתָּה הוּא מַלְכֵּנוּ, |
| a·ta hu Mo·shi·ei·nu. | אַתָּה הוּא מוֹשִׁיעֵנוּ. |

There is none like our God; there is none like our Lord; there is none like our King; there is none like our Savior.

Who is like our God? Who is like our Lord? Who is like our King? Who is like our Savior?

We will give thanks to our God; we will give thanks to our Lord; we will give thanks to our King; we will give thanks to our Savior.

Blessed is our God; blessed is our Lord; blessed is our King; blessed is our Savior.

You are our God; You are our Lord; You are our King; You are our Savior.

# EIN KEILOHEINU
## (Alternate Melody)

Medieval text

Boruch Karliner

**Majestically ( ♩ = 66)**

1. Ein kei- lo- hei - nu, ein ka-do- nei - nu,

ein ke-mal- kei - nu, ein ke-mo-shi ei - nu.

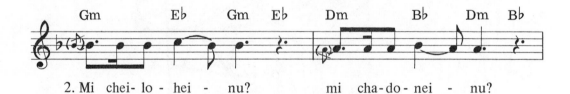

2. Mi chei- lo- hei - nu? mi cha-do- nei - nu?

mi che-mal- kei - nu? mi che-mo-shi-ei - nu?

3. No- deh lei-lo- hei - nu, no- deh la-do- nei - nu,

*D.C. (al Fine 5th time)*

no- deh le-mal- kei - nu, no- deh-le-mo-shi - ei - nu.

# ESA EINAI

Psalm 121:1

Shlomo Carlebach

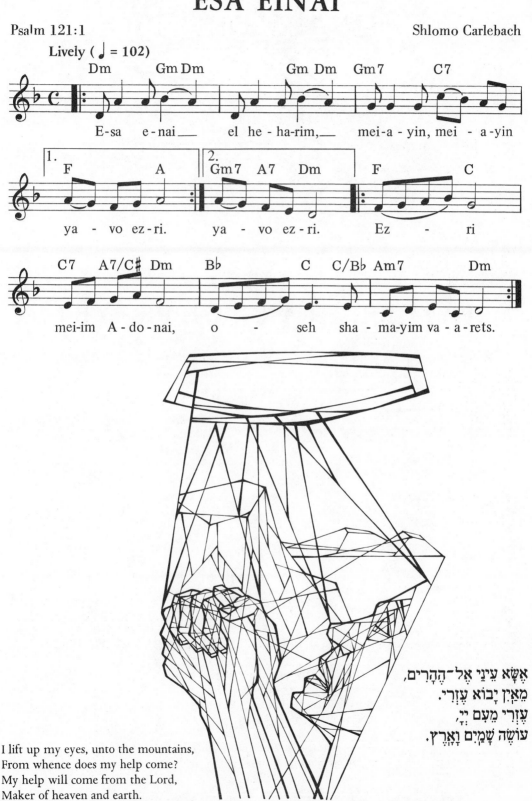

I lift up my eyes, unto the mountains,
From whence does my help come?
My help will come from the Lord,
Maker of heaven and earth.

אֶשָּׂא עֵינַי אֶל־הֶהָרִים,
מֵאַיִן יָבוֹא עֶזְרִי.
עֶזְרִי מֵעִם יְיָ,
עוֹשֵׂה שָׁמַיִם וָאָרֶץ.

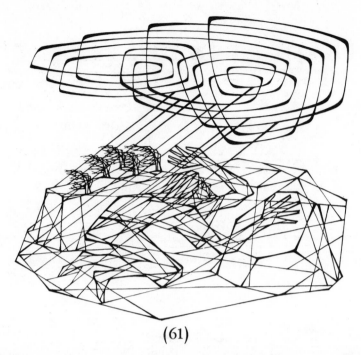

(61)

# FATHER, HEAR THE PRAYER

L. M. Willis

Adapted from *Eliyahu Hanavi*

Fervently ( ♩ = 66)

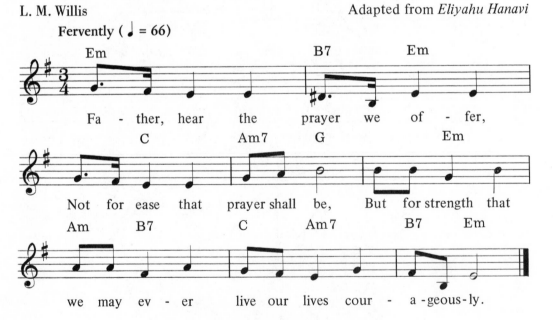

Father, hear the prayer we offer,
Not for ease that prayer shall be,
But for strength that we may ever
Live our lives courageously.

Be our strength in hours of weakness,
In our wanderings be our guide;
Through endeavor, failure, danger,
Be for ever at our side.

34

# FROM HEAVEN'S HEIGHTS
# THE THUNDER PEALS

Isaac M. Wise

Based on *Shavuot* mode

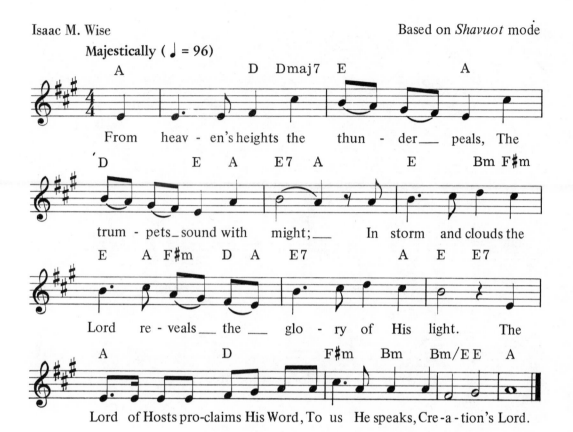

From heav-en's heights the thun-der___ peals, The trum-pets_sound with might;___ In storm and clouds the Lord re-veals___ the ___ glo-ry of His light. The Lord of Hosts pro-claims His Word, To us He speaks, Cre-a-tion's Lord.

The idols reel, their temples shake,
Despotic pow'rs rebound;
With awe the mountain summits quake,
Before the awful sound.
From Horeb's height descends the word,
To us He speaks, Creation's Lord.

Let Judah's harp intone His praise,
Our Maker's glory sing;
For truth and light, for heav'nly grace,
Reveal'd by God, our King.
Extol His name in one accord,
To us He speaks, Creation's Lord.

# GOD OF MIGHT

Composite text

Based on *Adir Hu*

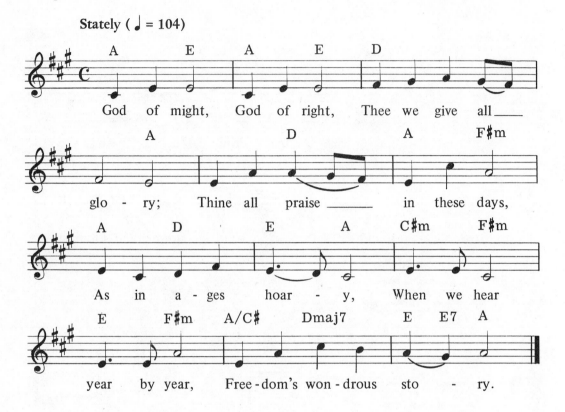

**Stately** ( ♩ = 104)

God of might, God of right, Thee we give all glo - ry; Thine all praise in these days, As in a - ges hoar - y, When we hear year by year, Free - dom's won - drous sto - ry.

Now as erst, when Thou first
Mads't the proclamation,
Warning loud ev'ry proud,
Ev'ry tyrant nation,
We Thy fame still proclaim,
Bow'd in adoration.

Be with all who in thrall
To their tasks are driven;
By Thy power speed the hour
When their chains are riven;
Earth around will resound
Joyful hymns to heaven.

## (69)
# GOD OF OUR PEOPLE

Daniel C. Roberts

George W. Warren

Martial ( ♩ = 112 )

God of our peo - ple, whose al - might - y hand

Leads forth in beau - ty all the star - ry band

Of shin - ing worlds in splen - dor through the skies,

Our grate - ful songs be - fore Thy throne a - rise.

Thy love divine hath led us in the past,
In this free land by Thee our lot is cast;
Be Thou our ruler, guardian, guide and stay,
Thy word our law, Thy paths our chosen way.

From war's alarms, from deadly pestilence,
Be Thy strong arm our ever sure defense;
Thy true religion in our hearts increase,
Thy bounteous goodness nourish us in peace.

Refresh Thy people on their toilsome way,
Lead us from night to never ending day;
Fill all our lives with love and grace divine,
And glory, laud and praise be ever Thine.

(p. 379)

# HALLELUHU, PRAISE HIM

Based on Psalm 150

Folk Melody

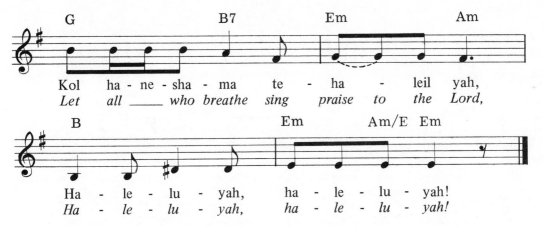

Kol ha - ne - sha - ma te - ha - leil yah,
*Let all ____ who breathe sing praise to the Lord,*

Ha - le - lu - yah, ha - le - lu - yah!
*Ha - le - lu - yah, ha - le - lu - yah!*

Praise Him, praise, with trumpet and drum, with strings and winds and voice;

Praise Him, praise, with song and with prayer, with joy, with dance, and with love.

Let all who breathe sing praise to the Lord, Halleluyah, Halleluyah!

Let all who breathe sing praise to the Lord, Halleluyah, Halleluyah!

הַלְלוּהוּ בְּצִלְצְלֵי־שָׁמַע,

Ha·le·lu·hu, ha·le·lu·hu,
be·tsil·tse·lei sha·ma.

הַלְלוּהוּ בְּצִלְצְלֵי תְרוּעָה.

Ha·le·lu·hu, ha·le·lu·hu,
be·tsil·tse·lei te·ru·a.

כֹּל הַנְּשָׁמָה תְּהַלֵּל יָהּ, הַלְלוּיָהּ!

Kol ha·ne·sha·ma te·ha·leil yah,
ha·le·lu·yah, ha·le·lu·yah!

כֹּל הַנְּשָׁמָה תְּהַלֵּל יָהּ, הַלְלוּיָהּ!

Kol ha·ne·sha·ma te·ha·leil yah,
ha·le·lu·yah, ha·le·lu·yah!

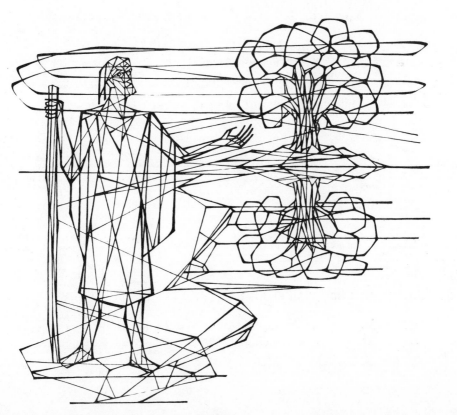

39

# HATIKVA

Naphtali Herz Imber

National Anthem of the
State of Israel

Stately ( ♩ = 76)

Kol od ba-lei-vav pe-ni - ma,

ne-fesh Ye-hu-di ho - mi - ya. U-le-

fa - tei miz-rach ka-di-ma, a-yin le-tsi-yon

tso-fi-ya. Od lo a-ve-da tik-va-tei - nu,

ha - tik-va she-not al-pa - yim, Li-he-yot am chof-shi

be - ar - tsei-nu, be-e-retz tsi-yon vi-ru-sha-la - yim.

Li-he-yot am chof - shi be-ar - tsei-nu, be-

e-retz tsi-yon vi-ru-sha-la - yim.

Kol od ba·lei·vav pe·ni·ma,

ne·fesh Ye·hu·di ho·mi·ya.

U·le·fa·a·tei miz·rach ka·di·ma,

a·yin le·tsi·yon tso·fi·ya.

Od lo a·ve·da tik·va·tei·nu,

ha·tik·va she·not al·pa·yim,

li·he·yot am chof·shi be·ar·tsei·nu,

be·e·rets tsi·yon vi·ru·sha·la·yim.

כָּל עוֹד בַּלֵּבָב פְּנִימָה

נֶפֶשׁ יְהוּדִי הוֹמִיָּה,

וּלְפַאֲתֵי מִזְרָח קָדִימָה

עַיִן לְצִיּוֹן צוֹפִיָּה.

עוֹד לֹא אָבְדָה תִקְוָתֵנוּ,

הַתִּקְוָה שְׁנוֹת אַלְפַּיִם,

לִהְיוֹת עַם חָפְשִׁי בְּאַרְצֵנוּ,

בְּאֶרֶץ צִיּוֹן וִירוּשָׁלָיִם.

So long as still within the inmost heart a Jewish spirit sings, so long as the eye looks eastward, gazing toward Zion, our hope is not lost — that hope of two millennia, to be a free people in our land, the land of Zion and Jerusalem.

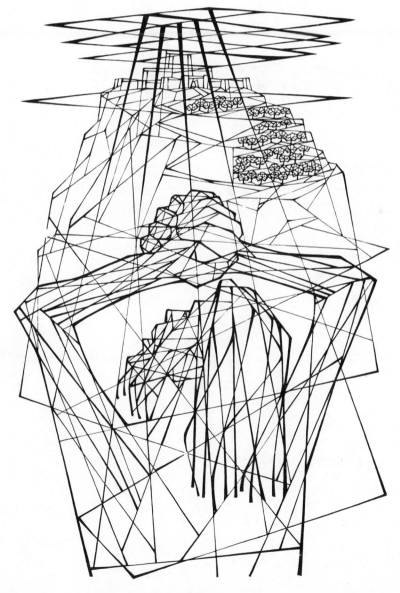

41

# HOSHIA ET AMECHA

Psalm 28:9

Chassidic Melody

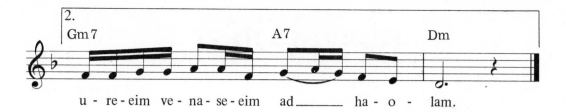

u - re - eim  ve - na - se - eim  ad_____ ha - o -  lam.

Ho·shl·a et a·me·cha

u·va·reich et na·cha·la·te·cha

u·re·eim ve·na·se·eim ad ha·o·lam.

הוֹשִׁיעָה אֶת־עַמֶּךָ

וּבָרֵךְ אֶת־נַחֲלָתֶךָ

וּרְעֵם וְנַשְּׂאֵם עַד־הָעוֹלָם.

Help Your people, bless Your heritage, tend them and exalt them for ever.

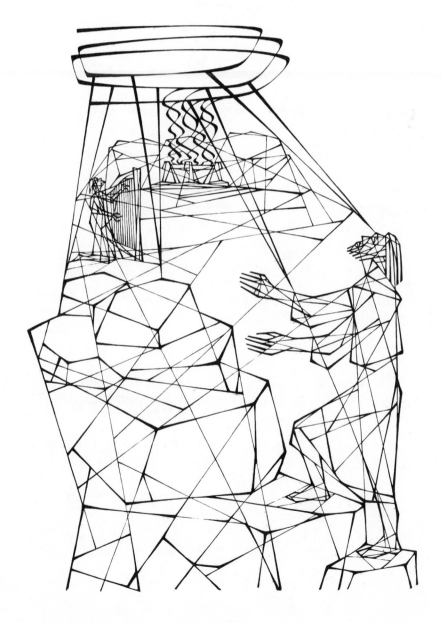

(Nos. 13 & 9)

# HOW GOOD IT IS

### (Alternate Melody for Lecha Dodi)

Florence Weisberg—Stanley R. Brav                    Louis Lewandowski

Flowingly ( ♩ = 100)

Le·cha do·di lik·rat ka·la

pe·nei Sha·bat ne·ka·be·la [2]

לְכָה דוֹדִי לִקְרַאת כַּלָּה,

פְּנֵי שַׁבָּת נְקַבְּלָה.

How good it is to thank the Lord,
To praise Your name, O God Most High;
To tell Your kindness through the day,
Your faithfulness when night draws nigh.

Le·cha do·di . . .

With joyous psalms and with the harp,
Will I Your marvels gladly sing;
Your works have made my heart rejoice;
I triumph in Your work, my King!

Le·cha do·di . . .

Like stately palm the righteous thrive,
As cedar fair they flourish free
In God's own house; His courts alone
Their dwelling-place and home shall be.

Le·cha do·di . . .

Still, in old age, ripe fruit they bear,
Verdant and fresh they still remain
To prove that God, my Rock of Help,
His righteousness does e'er maintain.

Le·cha do·di . . .

44

## (47)
# IF OUR GOD
# HAD NOT BEFRIENDED

Edward Churton (Based on Psalm 124)                    Jacob Weinberg

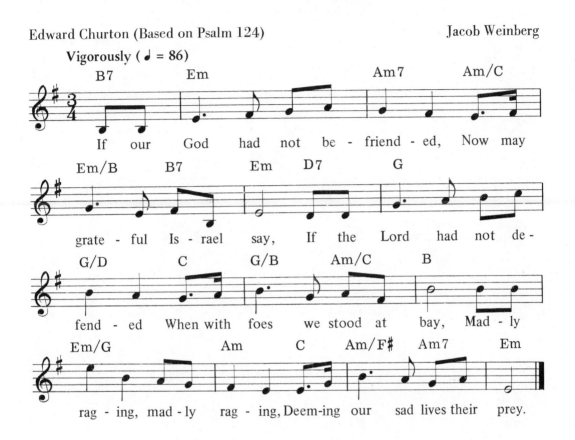

If our God had not befriended,
Now may grateful Israel say,
If the Lord had not defended
When with foes we stood at bay,
Madly raging, madly raging,
Deeming our sad lives their prey:

Then the tide of vengeful slaughters
O'er us had been seen to roll,
And their pride, like angry waters,

Had engulf'd our struggling soul,
Those loud waters, those loud waters,
Proud and spurning all control.

Praise to God, whose mercy token
Beam'd to still that raging sea;
Lo, the snare is rent and broken,
And our captive souls are free.
Lord of glory, Lord of glory,
Help can come alone from Thee.

45

# (42)
# IM EIN ANI LI MI LI?

Pirkei Avot 1:14

Folk Melody

Resolutely ( ♩ = 104)

Im ein a-ni li mi li?\_\_\_ U-che-she-a-
ni le-ats-mi ma a-ni? Ve - im lo ach-shav
ei - ma-tai, ei - ma - tai? Ve - im lo ach-shav
ei - ma-tai, ve-im lo ach-shav ei - ma-tai, ve-
im lo ach-shav ei-ma-tai, ei - ma-
tai? Ve - ei - ma - tai?

| Im ein a·ni li mi li? | אִם אֵין אֲנִי לִי מִי לִי? |
| U·che·she·a·ni le·ats·mi | וּכְשֶׁאֲנִי לְעַצְמִי |
| ma a·ni? | מָה אֲנִי? |
| Ve·im lo ach·shav ei·ma·tai, | וְאִם לֹא עַכְשָׁו אֵימָתַי, |
| ei·ma·tai? | אֵימָתַי? |

If I am not for myself, who will be for me? But if I am for myself alone, what
am I? And if not now, when?

47

# IN THE WILDERNESS

Judith K. Eisenstein

Based on *Akdamut* mode

Tenderly ( ♩ = 80)

In the wil-der-ness no wind blew,

In the heav-ens no bird flew,

In the mead-ows no cow was low-ing,

In the riv-ers the wa-ter stopped flow-ing.

Cam-el bells were no-where ring-ing,

E-ven the an-gels ceased their sing-ing.

O-ver the whole world si-lence was fall-ing,

On-ly the voice of the Sho-far call-ing.

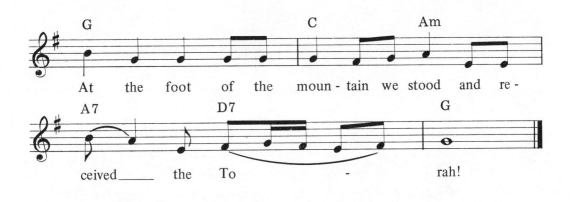

At the foot of the moun-tain we stood and re-ceived___ the To - rah!

# (36)

# IVEDU

Psalm 100:2

Folk Melody

Lively ( ♩ = 108)

I·ve·du et Ha·shem be·sim·cha,
bo·u le·fa·nav bi·re·na·na.

עִבְדוּ אֶת־ה׳ בְּשִׂמְחָה,
בֹּאוּ לְפָנָיו בִּרְנָנָה.

Serve the Lord with gladness! Come into His presence with singing!

# KI ESHMERA SHABBAT

Abraham Ibn Ezra, 12th C.

Sephardic Melody

Liltingly ( ♩ = 108)

Ki esh-me-ra Shab - bat, Eil _____ yish-me - rei - ni. Ki esh-me-ra Shab - bat Eil _____ yish-me - rei - ni. Ot hi le- o-le-mei_ ad bei - no u - vei - ni. Ot hi le- o-le-mei_ ad bei - no u - vei - ni.

Ki esh·me·ra Sha·bat
Eil ylsh·me·rei·ni.
Ot hi le·o·le·mei ad
bei·no u·vei·ni.

כִּי אֶשְׁמְרָה שַׁבָּת
אֵל יִשְׁמְרֵנִי.
אוֹת הִיא לְעָלְמֵי עַד
בֵּינוֹ וּבֵינִי.

If I keep Shabbat, God keeps me. It is a sign for ever between Him and me.

51

# LECHA DODI
## (Alternate Melody)

Liturgy, modified text                          Mordecai Zeira

**Liltingly** ($\downarrow$ = 72)

Le - cha  do - di __  lik - rat  ka - la,  lik - rat  ka - la,  pe -
nei  Sha - bat  ne - ka - be - la  ne - ka - be - la.  Le -
la  ne - ka - be - la.  Sha - bat  sha - lom,  Sha -
bat sha - lom, Sha - bat  sha - lom u - me - vo - rach. Sha  rach.

Beloved, come to meet the bride;
Beloved, come to greet Shabbat.
Shabbat peace and blessing.

| | |
|---|---|
| Le·cha do·di lik·rat ka·la,<br>pe·nei Sha·bat ne·ka·be·la. | לְכָה דוֹדִי לִקְרַאת כַּלָּה,<br>פְּנֵי שַׁבָּת נְקַבְּלָה. |

**1**

| | |
|---|---|
| Sha·mor ve·za·chor be·di·bur e·chad,<br>hish·mi·a·nu Eil ha·me·yu·chad.<br>A·do·nai e·chad u·she·mo e·chad,<br>le·sheim u·le·tif·e·ret ve·li·te·hi·la.<br><br>Le·cha do·di ... | שָׁמוֹר וְזָכוֹר בְּדִבּוּר אֶחָד,<br>הִשְׁמִיעָנוּ אֵל הַמְיֻחָד.<br>יְיָ אֶחָד וּשְׁמוֹ אֶחָד,<br>לְשֵׁם וּלְתִפְאֶרֶת וְלִתְהִלָּה.<br><br>לְכָה דוֹדִי ... |

**2**

| | |
|---|---|
| Lik·rat Sha·bat le·chu ve·nei·le·cha,<br>ki hi me·kor ha·be·ra·cha.<br>mei·rosh mi·ke·dem ne·su·cha,<br>sof ma·a·seh, be·ma·cha·sha·va<br>te·chi·la.<br><br>Le·cha do·di ... | לִקְרַאת שַׁבָּת לְכוּ וְנֵלְכָה,<br>כִּי הִיא מְקוֹר הַבְּרָכָה.<br>מֵרֹאשׁ מִקֶּדֶם נְסוּכָה,<br>סוֹף מַעֲשֶׂה, בְּמַחֲשָׁבָה תְּחִלָּה.<br><br>לְכָה דוֹדִי ... |

| | |
|---|---|
| 3 Mik·dash me·lech, ir me·lu·cha,<br>ku·mi tse·i mi·toch ha·ha·fei·cha.<br>rav lach she·vet be·ei·mek<br>   ha·ba·cha —<br>ve·hu ya·cha·mol a·la·yich chem·la.<br><br>Le·cha do·di . . . | 3 מִקְדַּשׁ מֶלֶךְ, עִיר מְלוּכָה,<br>קוּמִי צְאִי מִתּוֹךְ הַהֲפֵכָה.<br>רַב לָךְ שֶׁבֶת בְּעֵמֶק הַבָּכָא —<br>וְהוּא יַחֲמֹל עָלַיִךְ חֶמְלָה.<br><br>לְכָה דוֹדִי . . . |
| 4 Hit·na·a·ri! mei·a·far ku·mi!<br>li·ve·shi bi·ge·dei tif·ar·telch, a·mi!<br>al yad ben yi·shai, beit ha·lach·mi,<br>ka·re·va el naf·shi ge·a·la.<br><br>Le·cha do·di . . . | 4 הִתְנַעֲרִי! מֵעָפָר קוּמִי!<br>לִבְשִׁי בִּגְדֵי תִפְאַרְתֵּךְ, עַמִּי!<br>עַל־יַד בֶּן יִשַׁי, בֵּית הַלַּחְמִי,<br>קָרְבָה אֶל נַפְשִׁי גְאָלָה.<br><br>לְכָה דוֹדִי . . . |
| 5 Hit·o·re·ri, hit·o·re·ri,<br>ki va o·reich! ku·mi, o·ri,<br>u·ri u·ri, shir da·bei·ri;<br>ke·vod A·do·nai a·la·yich nig·la.<br><br>Le·cha do·di . . . | 5 הִתְעוֹרְרִי, הִתְעוֹרְרִי,<br>כִּי בָא אוֹרֵךְ! קוּמִי, אוֹרִי,<br>עוּרִי עוּרִי, שִׁיר דַּבֵּרִי;<br>כְּבוֹד יְיָ עָלַיִךְ נִגְלָה.<br><br>לְכָה דוֹדִי . . . |
| 6 Lo tei·vo·shi ve·lo ti·ka·le·mi;<br>ma tish·to·cha·chi, u·ma te·he·mi?<br>bach ye·che·su a·ni·yei a·mi,<br>ve·niv·ne·ta ir al ti·la.<br><br>Le·cha do·di . . . | 6 לֹא תֵבְשִׁי וְלֹא תִכָּלְמִי;<br>מַה תִּשְׁתּוֹחֲחִי, וּמַה תֶּהֱמִי?<br>בָּךְ יֶחֱסוּ עֲנִיֵּי עַמִּי,<br>וְנִבְנְתָה עִיר עַל תִּלָּהּ.<br><br>לְכָה דוֹדִי . . . |
| 7 Ve·ha·yu li·me·shi·sa sho·sa·yich,<br>ve·ra·cha·ku kol me·va·le·a·yich;<br>ya·sis a·la·yich E·lo·ha·yich,<br>ki·me·sos cha·tan al ka·la.<br><br>Le·cha do·di . . . | 7 וְהָיוּ לִמְשִׁסָּה שֹׁאסָיִךְ,<br>וְרָחֲקוּ כָּל־מְבַלְּעָיִךְ;<br>יָשִׂישׂ עָלַיִךְ אֱלֹהָיִךְ,<br>כִּמְשׂוֹשׂ חָתָן עַל כַּלָּה.<br><br>לְכָה דוֹדִי . . . |
| 8 Ya·min u·se·mol tif·ro·tsi,<br>ve·et A·do·nai ta·a·ri·tsi:<br>al yad ish ben par·tsi,<br>ve·nis·me·cha ve·na·gi·la!<br><br>Le·cha do·di . . . | 8 יָמִין וּשְׂמֹאל תִּפְרֹצִי,<br>וְאֶת יְיָ תַּעֲרִיצִי:<br>עַל יַד אִישׁ בֶּן פַּרְצִי,<br>וְנִשְׂמְחָה וְנָגִילָה!<br><br>לְכָה דוֹדִי . . . |
| 9 Bo·i ve·sha·lom, a·te·ret ba·a·la;<br>gam be·sim·cha u·ve·tso·ho·la.<br>toch e·mu·nei am se·gu·la.<br>bo·i cha·la! bo·i cha·la!<br><br>Le·cha do·di . . . | 9 בּוֹאִי בְשָׁלוֹם, עֲטֶרֶת בַּעְלָהּ;<br>גַּם בְּשִׂמְחָה וּבְצָהֳלָה.<br>תּוֹךְ אֱמוּנֵי עַם סְגֻלָּה.<br>בּוֹאִי כַלָּה! בּוֹאִי כַלָּה!<br><br>לְכָה דוֹדִי . . . |

*The translation of Lecha Dodi is on page 123.*

*See "How Good It Is" Page 44

# LO YISA GOI

Isaiah 2:4

Folk Melody

Lo yi·sa goi el goi che·rev,
lo yil·me·du od mil·cha·ma.

לֹא יִשָּׂא גוֹי אֶל גּוֹי חֶרֶב,
לֹא יִלְמְדוּ עוֹד מִלְחָמָה.

Nation shall not lift up sword against nation, nor ever again shall they train for war.

# MAGEIN AVOT

Liturgy

Israel and Samuel E. Goldfarb

57

Ma·gein a·vot bi·de·va·ro,

me·cha·yei ha·kol be·ma·a·ma·ro.

Ha·eil ha·ka·dosh she·ein ka·mo·hu.

ha·mei·ni·ach le·a·mo be·yom Sha·bat
    kod·sho,
ki vam ra·tsa le·ha·ni·ach la·hem.

Le·fa·nav na·a·vod be·yir·a va·fa·chad,

ve·no·deh li·she·mo be·chol
    yom ta·mid
mei·ein ha·be·ra·chot.

Eil ha·ho·da·ot, A·don ha·sha·lom,

me·ka·deish ha·sha·bat u·me·va·reich
    she·vi·i,
u·mei·ni·ach bi·ke·du·sha le·am
    me·du·she·nei o·neg,
zei·cher le·ma·a·sei ve·rei·shit.

מָגֵן אָבוֹת בִּדְבָרוֹ,

מְחַיֶּה הַכֹּל בְּמַאֲמָרוֹ.

הָאֵל הַקָּדוֹשׁ, שֶׁאֵין כָּמוֹהוּ,

הַמֵּנִיחַ לְעַמּוֹ בְּיוֹם שַׁבַּת קָדְשׁוֹ,

כִּי בָם רָצָה לְהָנִיחַ לָהֶם.

לְפָנָיו נַעֲבוֹד בְּיִרְאָה וָפַחַד,

וְנוֹדֶה לִשְׁמוֹ בְּכָל־יוֹם תָּמִיד,

מֵעֵין הַבְּרָכוֹת.

אֵל הַהוֹדָאוֹת, אֲדוֹן הַשָּׁלוֹם,

מְקַדֵּשׁ הַשַּׁבָּת וּמְבָרֵךְ שְׁבִיעִי,

וּמֵנִיחַ בִּקְדֻשָּׁה לְעַם מְדֻשְּׁנֵי עֹנֶג,

זֵכֶר לְמַעֲשֵׂה בְרֵאשִׁית.

# (38)
# MA NAVU

Isaiah 52:7

Joseph Spivak

1. Ma na - vu al he - ha - rim ra - ge - lei____ me - va -
2. Kol tso - fa·yich na - se - u kol, yach - dav____ ye - ra -

seir,_____ Ma na - vu al he - ha - rim ra - ge -
nei - nu, Kol tso - fa·yich na - se - u kol, yach -

lei____ me - va - seir____ mash - mi - a
dav____ ye - ra - nei - nu. Ki____ a - yin be - a - yin

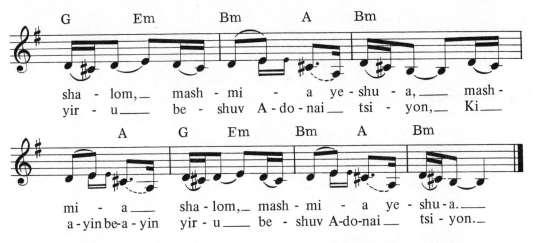

shalom,___ mash-mi — a ye-shu-a,___ mash-
yir-u___ be - shuv A-do-nai___ tsi - yon,___ Ki___

mi - a___ sha-lom, mash-mi-a ye-shu-a.___
a-yin be-a-yin yir-u___ be - shuv A-do-nai___ tsi - yon.___

| | |
|---|---|
| Ma na·vu al he·ha·rim | מַה־נָּאווּ עַל־הֶהָרִים |
| ra·ge·lei me·va·seir | רַגְלֵי מְבַשֵּׂר |
| mash·mi·a sha·lom, | מַשְׁמִיעַ שָׁלוֹם, |
| mash·mi·a ye·shu·a. | מַשְׁמִיעַ יְשׁוּעָה. |
| Kol tso·fa·yich na·se·u kol, | קוֹל צֹפַיִךְ נָשְׂאוּ קוֹל, |
| yach·dav ye·ra·nei·nu. | יַחְדָּו יְרַנֵּנוּ. |
| Ki a·yin be·a·yin yir·u | כִּי עַיִן בְּעַיִן יִרְאוּ |
| be·shuv A·do·nai tsi·yon. | בְּשׁוּב יְיָ צִיּוֹן. |

How beautiful upon the mountains are the feet of the herald, the one who
proclaims peace, who brings tidings of good and proclaims deliverance. All
your sentries raise their voices and shout together in triumph. For clearly
they see the return of the Lord to Zion.

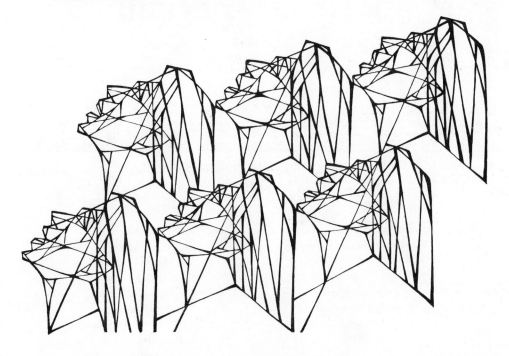

# MAOZ TSUR
# ROCK OF AGES

Hebrew: Mordechai 13th C
English: Marcus Jastrow, Gustave Gottheil
Adapted from the German of Leopold Stein

Ashkenazic folk melody

Kindling new the holy lamps,
Priests approved in suffering,
Purified the nation's shrines,
Brought to God their offering.
And His courts surrounding
Hear, in joy abounding,
  Happy throngs,
  Singing songs,
With a mighty sounding.

Children of the Maccabees,
Whether free or fettered,
Wake the echoes of the songs,
Where you may be scattered.
Yours the message cheering,
That the time is nearing,
  Which will see
  All men free,
Tyrants disappearing.

Mordechai, 13th C.
Majestically ( ♩= 96)

Venetian-melody, as transcribed by
Benedetto Marcello

Ma - oz tsur ye - shu - a - ti, _____ le-cha _____ na - eh le - sha - bei - ach;

ti - kon beit te - fi - la - ti, _____ ve-sham _____ to - da ne - za - bei - ach.

Le - eit ta - chin mat - bei - ach, mi - tsar _____ ha - me - na - bei - ach, az _____ eg - mor, be-shir miz - mor, _____ cha - nu - kat ha - miz - bei - ach.

|  |  |
|---|---|
| Ma·oz tsur ye·shu·a·ti, | מָעוֹז צוּר יְשׁוּעָתִי, |
| le·cha na·eh le·sha·bei·ach; | לְךָ נָאֶה לְשַׁבֵּחַ; |
| ti·kon beit te·fi·la·ti, | תִּכּוֹן בֵּית תְּפִלָּתִי, |
| ve·sham to·da ne·za·bei·ach. | וְשָׁם תּוֹדָה נְזַבֵּחַ. |
| Le·eit ta·chin mat·bei·ach, | לְעֵת תָּכִין מַטְבֵּחַ, |
| mi·tsar ha·me·na·bei·ach, | מִצָּר הַמְנַבֵּחַ, |
| az eg·mor, be·shir miz·mor, | אָז אֶגְמוֹר, בְּשִׁיר מִזְמוֹר, |
| cha·nu·kat ha·miz·bei·ach. | חֲנֻכַּת הַמִּזְבֵּחַ. |

# MENUCHA VESIMCHA

Text by Mose

Folk Melody

| | |
|---|---|
| Me·nu·cha ve·sim·cha or la·ye·hu·dim, | מְנוּחָה וְשִׂמְחָה אוֹר לַיְּהוּדִים, |
| yom sha·ba·ton yom ma·cha·ma·dim. | יוֹם שַׁבָּתוֹן יוֹם מַחֲמַדִּים. |
| Sho·me·rav ve·zo·che·rav hei·ma me·i·dim, | שׁוֹמְרָיו וְזוֹכְרָיו הֵמָּה מְעִידִים, |
| ki le·shi·sha kol be·ru·im ve·o·me·dim. | כִּי לְשִׁשָּׁה כֹּל בְּרוּאִים וְעוֹמְדִים. |
| She·mei sha·ma·yim e·rets ve·ya·mim, | שְׁמֵי שָׁמַיִם אֶרֶץ וְיַמִּים, |
| kol tse·va ma·rom ge·vo·him ve·ra·mim. | כָּל־צְבָא מָרוֹם גְּבוֹהִים וְרָמִים. |
| ta·nin ve·a·dam ve·cha·yat re·ei·mim, | תַּנִּין וְאָדָם וְחַיַּת רְאֵמִים, |
| ki ve·yah A·do·nai tsur o·la·mim. | כִּי בְּיָהּ יְיָ צוּר עוֹלָמִים. |

Rest and gladness, a light for the Jew, the Sabbath day is a day of delight.
Those who keep and remember it give witness to the story of creation. All
things were made: the highest heavens, earth and sea, the high and exalted
host of heaven, sea-monster and human, the wild beast — the Lord God is
the Creator of all worlds.

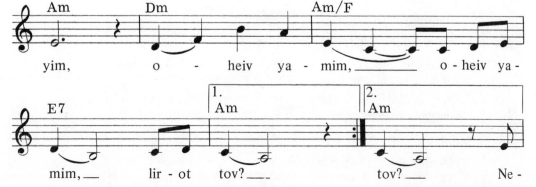

## (34)

# MI HA-ISH

Psalm 34:13-15

Chassidic Melody

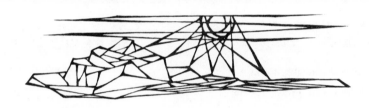

Lyrically (♩ = 86)

Mi ____ ha - ish ____ he - cha - feits cha-
yim, o - heiv ya - mim, ____ o - heiv ya-
mim, ____ lir - ot tov? ____ tov? ____ Ne -

63

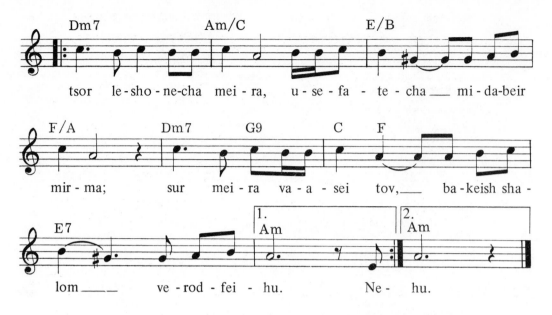

tsor le-sho-ne-cha mei-ra, u-se-fa-te-cha mi-da-beir mir-ma; sur mei-ra va-a-sei tov, ba-keish sha-lom ve-rod-fei-hu. Ne- hu.

Mi ha·ish he·cha·feits cha·yim,
o·heiv ya·mim, lir·ot tov?

מִי הָאִישׁ הֶחָפֵץ חַיִּים,
אֹהֵב יָמִים, לִרְאוֹת טוֹב?

Ne·tsor le·sho·ne·cha mei·ra,
u·se·fa·te·cha mi·da·beir mir·ma;

נְצֹר לְשׁוֹנְךָ מֵרָע,
וּשְׂפָתֶיךָ מִדַּבֵּר מִרְמָה;

sur mei·ra va·a·sei tov,
ba·keish sha·lom ve·rod·fei·hu.

סוּר מֵרָע וַעֲשֵׂה טוֹב,
בַּקֵּשׁ שָׁלוֹם וְרָדְפֵהוּ.

Who among you loves life, and longs to enjoy good for many days? Then guard your tongue from evil, and your lips from deceitful speech; turn away from evil, and do good; seek peace and pursue it.

## (55)
# MI YEMALEIL

Hebrew: author unknown
English: Judith K. Eisenstein and others.

Menashe Ravina

Joyously ( ♩ = 92)

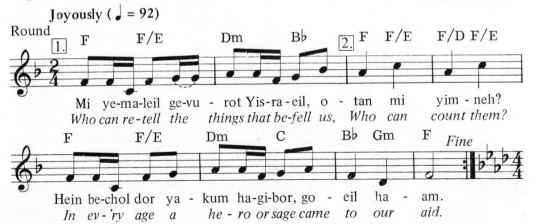

Mi ye-ma-leil ge-vu - rot Yis-ra-eil, o - tan mi yim - neh?
*Who can re-tell the things that be-fell us, Who can count them?*

Hein be-chol dor ya - kum ha-gi-bor, go - eil ha - am.
*In ev-'ry age a he - ro or sage came to our aid.*

64

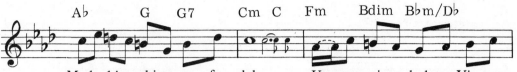

She-ma! Ba - ya-mim ha-heim ba- ze-man ha - zeh,
*Hark! In days of yore, in Is - ra-el's an-cient land,— Brave*

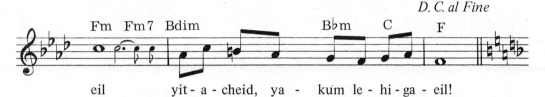

Ma-ka-bimo-shi-a u - fo - deh. U-ve-ya-mei - nu kol am Yis-ra-
*Mac-ca-be-us led his faith-ful band. And now all Is - rael must as one a-*

D. C. al Fine

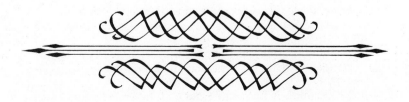

eil yit-a - cheid, ya - kum le - hi - ga - eil!
*rise, —— Re-deem it - self through deed and sac - ri - fice!*

Mi ye-ma-leil ge-vu-rot Yis-ra-eil,
o-tan mi yim-neh?

Hein be-chol dor ya-kum ha-gi-bor,
go-eil ha-am.

She-ma! Ba-ya-mim ha-heim
    ba-ze-man ha-zeh,
Ma-ka-bi mo-shi-a u-fo-deh.

U-ve-ya-mei-nu kol am Yis-ra-eil

yit-a-cheid, ya-kum le-hi-ga-eil!

מִי יְמַלֵּל גְּבוּרוֹת יִשְׂרָאֵל,
אוֹתָן מִי יִמְנֶה?

הֵן בְּכָל דּוֹר יָקוּם הַגִּבּוֹר,
גּוֹאֵל הָעָם.

שְׁמַע! בַּיָּמִים הָהֵם בַּזְּמַן הַזֶּה
מַכַּבִּי מוֹשִׁיעַ וּפוֹדֶה.
וּבְיָמֵינוּ כָּל עַם יִשְׂרָאֵל
יִתְאַחֵד יָקוּם לְהִגָּאֵל!

Who can retell the things that befell us,
Who can count them?
In every age a hero or sage
Came to our aid.

Hark! In days of yore, in Israel's ancient land,
Brave Maccabeus led his faithful band.
And now all Israel must as one arise,
Redeem itself through deed and sacrifice!

65

# O GOD, OUR HELP

Isaac Watts (based on Psalm 90)                                    William Croft

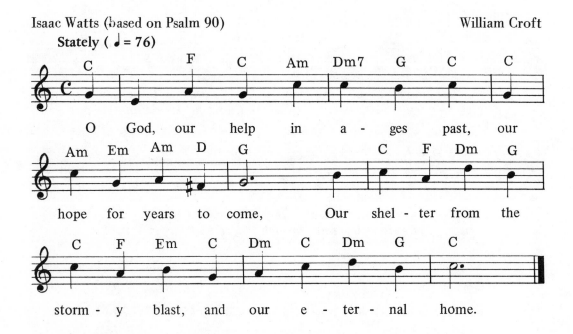

O God, our help in ages past, our hope for years to come,
Our shelter from the stormy blast, and our eternal home.

Before the hills in order stood, or earth received her frame,
From everlasting You are God, to endless years the same.

Beneath the shadow of Your throne Your children dwell secure;
Sufficient is Your arm alone, and our defence is sure.

O God, our help in ages past, our hope for years to come,
Be now our guide while troubles last, and our eternal home.

## (12)
# O HOLY SABBATH DAY

Isaac S. Moses

Jacob Beimel
(based on *Magein Avot* mode)

Solemnly ( ♩ = 92)

O holy Sabbath day, draw near, You are the source of bliss and cheer; The first in God's cre - a - tive thought, The fi - nal aim of all He wrought. Wel - come, wel - come, day of rest, Day of joy the Lord has blessed.

O holy Sabbath day, draw near,
You are the source of bliss and cheer;
The first in God's creative thought,
The final aim of all He wrought.

   Welcome, welcome, day of rest,
   Day of joy the Lord has blessed.

Let all rejoice with all their might,
The Sabbath, freedom brings and light;
Let songs of praise to God ascend,
And voices sweet in chorus blend.

   Welcome, welcome, day of rest,
   Day of joy the Lord has blessed.

Now come, O blessed Sabbath-Bride,
Our joy, our comfort, and our pride;
All cares and sorrow now bid cease,
And fill our waiting hearts with peace.

   Welcome, welcome, day of rest,
   Day of joy the Lord has blessed.

# (63)
# O LORD, WHERE SHALL I FIND YOU?

Judah Ben Samuel Halevi                                      Jacob Weinberg

O, how shall mortals praise You, when angels strive in vain —
Or build for You a dwelling, whom worlds cannot contain?
I find You in the marvels of Your creative might,
In visions in Your temple, in dreams that bless the night.

Who say they have not seen You, Your heavens refute their word;
Their hosts declare Your glory, though never voice be heard.
And You, transcendent, holy, delight in Your creatures' praise,
And descend where we are gathered to glorify Your ways.

## (65)
# O WORSHIP THE KING

Robert Grant (Based on Psalm 104)                    J. Michael Haydn

Lively ( ♩ = 120)

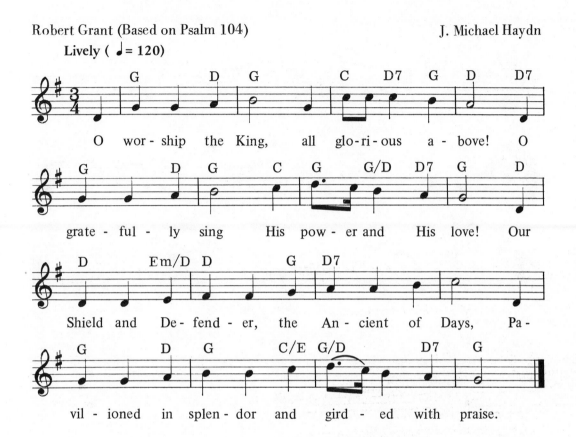

O worship the King, all glorious above! O
gratefully sing His power and His love! Our
Shield and Defender, the Ancient of Days, Pavilioned in splendor and girded with praise.

O worship the King, all glorious above!
O gratefully sing His pow'r and His love!
Our Shield and Defender, the Ancient of Days,
Pavilioned in splendor and girded with praise.

O tell of His might, O sing of His grace,
Whose robe is the light, whose canopy space!
His chariots of wrath the deep thunderclouds form,
And dark is His path on the wings of the storm.

The earth, with its stores of wonders untold,
Almighty, Your power has founded of old;

Has 'stablished it fast by a changeless decree,
And 'round it has cast, like a mantle, the sea.

Your bountiful care what tongue can recite?
It breathes in the air, it shines in the light,
It streams from the hills, it descends to the plain,
And sweetly distils in the dew and the rain.

Frail children of dust, and feeble as frail,
In You do we trust, nor find You to fail;
Your mercies how tender, how firm to the end,
Our Maker, Defender, Redeemer and Friend!

## (37)
# PITECHU LI

Psalm 118:19

Jacob Beimel

Pi - te - chu ___ li sha - a - rei tse - dek,
a - vo vam, o - deh ___ Yah. Pi - te - chu ___ li sha - a -
rei tse - dek, a - vo vam o - deh ___ Yah.
Pi - te - chu li sha - a - rei tse - dek, a - vo
vam o - deh ___ Yah. ___ Pi - te - chu li sha - a -
rei tse - dek, a - vo vam o - deh ___ Yah.

Pi·te·chu li

sha·a·rei tse·dek

a·vo vam, o·deh Yah.

פִּתְחוּ־לִי

שַׁעֲרֵי־צֶדֶק

אָבֹא־בָם, אוֹדֶה יָהּ.

Open for me the gates of righteousness; I will enter them and give thanks
to the Lord.

70

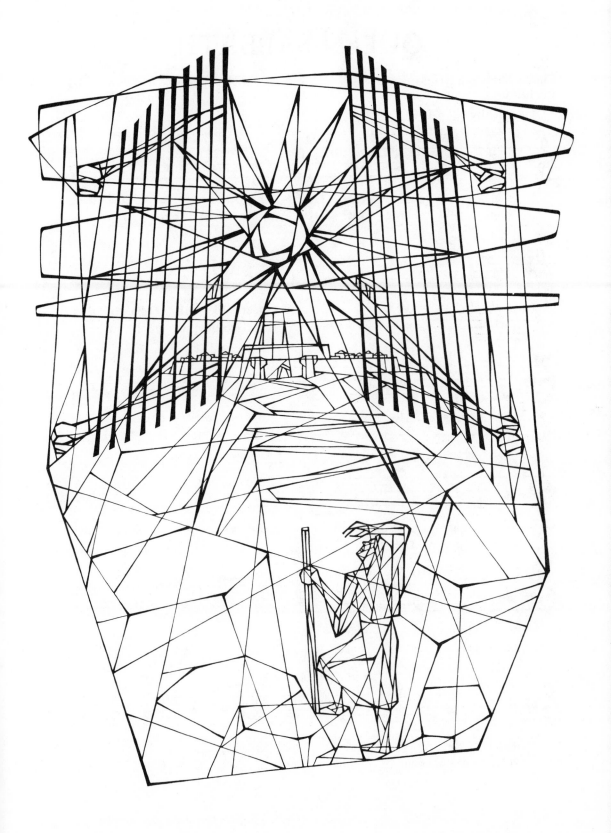

# (6)
# QUEEN SABBATH

Chaim Nachman Bialik
English by A. Irma Cohon

Pinchos Minkowsky

Ha - cha - ma mei - rosh ha - i - la - not nis -
The sun on the tree - tops no long - er is

tal - le - ka, Bo - u ve - nei - tsei lik - rat Sha - bat ha -
seen.___ Come ga - ther to wel - come the Sab - bath, our

mal - ka. Hi - nei hi yo - re - det, ha - ke -
queen.___ Be - hold her de - scend - ing the

do - sha ha - be - ru - cha, Ve - i - ma mal -
ho - ly the blessed,___ And with her the

a - chim, tse - va sha - lom u - me - nu - cha. Bo -
an - gels of peace and of rest.___ Draw

i, bo - i ha - mal___ ka! Bo -
near, draw near, and here___ a - bide, Draw

Am    Dm    G    C

i,    bo - i    ha - ka - - la!    Sha-
near,  draw  near,  O  Sab - bath  bride.  Peace

C7    F    Bb    C  C7  F

lom a - lei - chem,— mal - a - chei___ ha - sha - lom.
al - so  to  you,—  you___ an - gels  of  peace.

Ha·cha·ma mel·rosh ha·i·la·not  
nls·tal·le·ka.  
Bo·u ve·nel·tsel llk·rat Sha·bat  
ha·mal·ka.  
Hl·nel hl yo·re·det, ha·ke·do·sha  

ha·be·ru·cha,  

Ve·l·ma mal·a·chim, tse·va sha·lom  

u·me·nu·cha.  

Bo·l, bo·l ha·mal·ka!  

Bo·l, bo·l ha·ka·la!  

Sha·lom a·lel·chem, mal·a·chei  
ha·sha·lom.

הַחַמָּה מֵרֹאשׁ הָאִילָנוֹת נִסְתַּלְּקָה,

בֹּאוּ וְנֵצֵא לִקְרַאת שַׁבָּת הַמַּלְכָּה.

הִנֵּה הִיא יוֹרֶדֶת, הַקְּדוֹשָׁה

הַבְּרוּכָה,

וְעִמָּהּ מַלְאָכִים, צְבָא שָׁלוֹם

וּמְנוּחָה.

בֹּאִי, בֹּאִי הַמַּלְכָּה!

בֹּאִי, בֹּאִי הַכַּלָּה!

שָׁלוֹם עֲלֵיכֶם מַלְאֲכֵי הַשָּׁלוֹם.

The sun on the treetops no longer is seen,  
Come gather to welcome the Sabbath, our queen.  
Behold her descending, the holy, the blessed,  
And with her the angels of peace and of rest.  
    Draw near, draw near, and here abide,  
    Draw near, draw near, O Sabbath bride.  
Peace also to you, you angels of peace.

# RAD HALAILA
## (Hora Mechudeshet)

Yaakov Orland                                                    Chassidic Melody

Lively ( ♩ = 122)

Rad ha-lai-la rav shi-rei-nu,

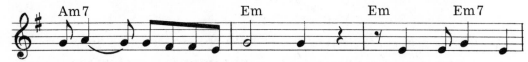

ha-bo___kei-a la-sha-ma-yim.          Shu-vi shu-vi

ho-ra-tei-nu me-chu-de-shet shiv-a-ta-yim.

Shu-vi shu-vi ve-na-sov ki dar-kei-nu ein la sof,

ki od nim-she-chet ha-shal-she-let,

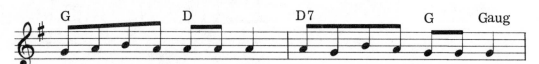

ki li-bei-nu leiv e-chad mi-ni az va-a-dei ad

ki od nim-she-chet ha-shal-she-let.

Rad ha-lal-la rav shi-rei-nu,
ha-bo-kei-a la-sha-ma-yim.
Shu-vi shu-vi ho-ra-tei-nu
me-chu-de-shet shiv-a-ta-yim.

רַד הַלַּיְלָה רַב שִׁירֵנוּ,
הַבּוֹקֵעַ לַשָּׁמָיִם.
שׁוּבִי שׁוּבִי הוֹרָתֵנוּ
מְחוּדֶשֶׁת שִׁבְעָתָיִם.

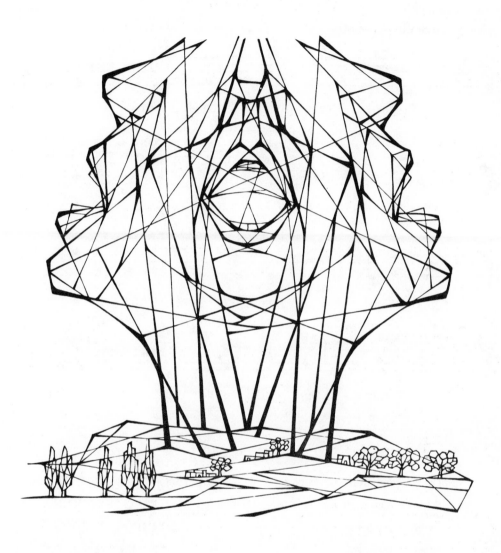

| | |
|---|---|
| Shu·vi shu·vi ve·na·sov | שׁוּבִי שׁוּבִי וְנָסוֹב |
| ki dar·kei·nu ein la sof, | כִּי דַרְכֵּנוּ אֵין לָהּ סוֹף, |
| ki od nim·she·chet ha·shal·she·let, | כִּי עוֹד נִמְשֶׁכֶת הַשַּׁלְשֶׁלֶת, |
| ki li·bei·nu leiv e·chad | כִּי לִבֵּנוּ לֵב אֶחָד |
| mi·ni az va·a·dei ad | מִינִי אָז וַעֲדֵי עַד |
| ki od nim·she·chet ha·shal·she·let. | כִּי עוֹד נִמְשֶׁכֶת הַשַּׁלְשֶׁלֶת. |
| La, la la, la la la la la la . . . . . | ל, ל, ל, ל, ל, ל, ל, . . . . |

Night descends, and great is our song which breaks through to the heavens. Again, again our Hora, renewed sevenfold. Again, again, and let us go around. For our path has no end; for the chain still continues. For our heart is one heart, now and always, for the chain still continues.

(p. 690)

# SACHAKI, SACHAKI

Saul Tchernichowsky

T. Shlonsky

Dreamily ( ♩ = 60)

Sa-cha-ki, sa-cha-ki, al ha-cha-lo-mot, zu a-ni ha-cho-lem sach, Sa-cha-ki ki va-a-dam a-a-min Ki o-de-ni___ ma-a-min bach. Sa-cha-ki ki va-a-dam a-a-min Ki o-de-ni___ ma-a-min bach.

| Laugh, laugh at all my dreams! | שַׂחֲקִי, שַׂחֲקִי עַל הַחֲלוֹמוֹת, |
| What I dream shall yet come true! | זוּ אֲנִי הַחוֹלֵם שָׂח, |
| Laugh at my belief in man, | שַׂחֲקִי כִּי בְאָדָם אַאֲמִין, |
| At my belief in you. | כִּי עוֹדֶנִּי מַאֲמִין בָּךְ. |
|  |  |
| Freedom still my soul demands, | כִּי עוֹד נַפְשִׁי דְּרוֹר שׁוֹאֶפֶת, |
| Unbartered for a calf of gold. | לֹא מְכַרְתִּיהָ לְעֵגֶל פָּז, |
| For still I do believe in man, | כִּי עוֹד אַאֲמִין גַּם בָּאָדָם, |
| And in his spirit, strong and bold. | גַּם בְּרוּחוֹ, רוּחַ עָז. |
|  |  |
| And in the future I still believe — | אַאֲמִינָה גַּם בֶּעָתִיד, |
| Though it be distant, come it will — | אַף אִם יִרְחַק זֶה הַיּוֹם. |
| When nations shall each other bless, | אַךְ בֹּא יָבוֹא — יִשְׂאוּ שָׁלוֹם |
| And peace at last the earth shall fill. | אָז וּבְרָכָה לְאֹם מִלְאֹם. |

❖ ❖

# (26)
# SHACHAR AVAKESHECHA

Solomon ibn Gabirol

Isadore Freed

| | |
|---|---|
| Sha·char a·va·ke·she·cha, tsu·ri | שַׁחַר אֲבַקֶּשְׁךָ, צוּרִי |
| u·mis·ga·bi, | וּמִשְׂגַּבִּי, |
| e·roch le·fa·ne·cha shach·ri | אֶעֱרוֹךְ לְפָנֶיךָ שַׁחְרִי |
| ve·gam ar·bi. | וְגַם עַרְבִּי. |
| Lif·nei ge·du·la·te·cha e·mod | לִפְנֵי גְדֻלָּתְךָ אֶעֱמֹד |
| ve·e·ba·heil | וְאֶבָּהֵל, |
| ki ei·ne·cha tir·eh kol | כִּי עֵינְךָ תִרְאֶה כָל |
| mach·she·vot li·bi. | מַחְשְׁבוֹת לִבִּי. |
| Ma zeh a·sher yu·chal | מַה־זֶּה אֲשֶׁר יוּכַל |
| ha·leiv ve·ha·la·shon | הַלֵּב וְהַלָּשׁוֹן |
| la·a·sot, u·ma ko·ach ru·chi | לַעֲשׂוֹת, וּמַה כֹּחַ רוּחִי |
| be·toch kir·bi? | בְּתוֹךְ קִרְבִּי? |
| Hi·nei le·cha ti·tav zim·rat | הִנֵּה לְךָ תִּיטַב זִמְרַת |
| enosh. Al kein | אֱנוֹשׁ. עַל כֵּן |
| o·de·cha be·od ti·he·yeh | אוֹדְךָ בְּעוֹד תִּהְיֶה |
| nish·mat E·lo·ah bi. | נִשְׁמַת אֱלוֹהַּ בִּי. |

At dawn I seek You, my Rock and Stronghold; I place before You my morning and evening prayers. Before Your greatness I stand afraid, for Your eye sees all my thoughts. What can heart and tongue do, and what is my spirit's strength within me? Behold, our human song will gain Your favor. Therefore I will affirm You while yet Your spirit lives within me.

# (8)
# SHALOM ALEICHEM

Kabbalistic Zemira, 17th C.　　　　　　　　Israel Goldfarb

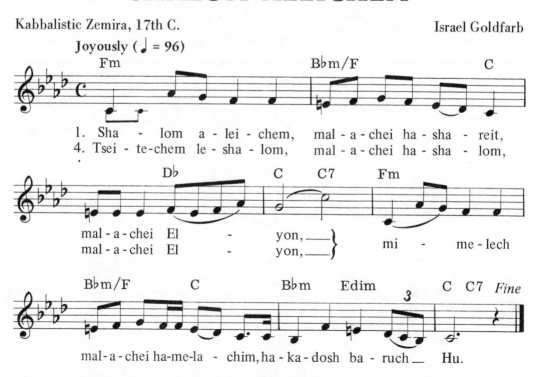

2. Bo - a-chem le-sha - lom, mal-a-chei ha-sha - lom,
   chu - ni le-sha - lom, mal-a-chei ha-sha - lom,

mal-a - chei _ El - yon,                    mi - me - lech
mal-a - chei _ El - yon,

mal-a-chei ha-me-la - chim, ha - ka-dosh ba-ruch  Hu. 3. Ba-re - Hu.

| | |
|---|---|
| Sha·lom a·lei·chem, mal·a·chei ha·sha·reit, mal·a·chei El·yon, | שָׁלוֹם עֲלֵיכֶם, מַלְאֲכֵי הַשָּׁרֵת, מַלְאֲכֵי עֶלְיוֹן, |
| mi·me·lech ma·le·chei ha·me·la·chim, | מִמֶּלֶךְ מַלְכֵי הַמְּלָכִים, |
| ha·ka·dosh ba·ruch Hu. | הַקָּדוֹשׁ בָּרוּךְ הוּא. |
| Bo·a·chem le·sha·lom, mal·a·chei ha·sha·lom, mal·a·chei El·yon, | בּוֹאֲכֶם לְשָׁלוֹם, מַלְאֲכֵי הַשָּׁלוֹם, מַלְאֲכֵי עֶלְיוֹן, |
| mi·me·lech ma·le·chei ha·me·la·chim, | מִמֶּלֶךְ מַלְכֵי הַמְּלָכִים, |
| ha·ka·dosh ba·ruch Hu. | הַקָּדוֹשׁ בָּרוּךְ הוּא. |
| Ba·re·chu·ni le·sha·lom, mal·a·chei ha·sha·lom, mal·a·chei El·yon, | בָּרְכוּנִי לְשָׁלוֹם, מַלְאֲכֵי הַשָּׁלוֹם, מַלְאֲכֵי עֶלְיוֹן, |
| mi·me·lech ma·le·chei ha·me·la·chim, | מִמֶּלֶךְ מַלְכֵי הַמְּלָכִים, |
| ha·ka·dosh ba·ruch Hu. | הַקָּדוֹשׁ בָּרוּךְ הוּא. |
| Tsei·te·chem le·sha·lom, mal·a·chei ha·sha·lom, mal·a·chei El·yon, | צֵאתְכֶם לְשָׁלוֹם, מַלְאֲכֵי הַשָּׁלוֹם, מַלְאֲכֵי עֶלְיוֹן, |
| mi·me·lech ma·le·chei ha·me·la·chim, | מִמֶּלֶךְ מַלְכֵי הַמְּלָכִים, |
| ha·ka·dosh ba·ruch Hu. | הַקָּדוֹשׁ בָּרוּךְ הוּא. |

# (31)
# SHOMEIR YISRAEIL

Liturgy

Israel Goldfarb

o-me-rim, ha - o-me-rim she-ma Yis-ra - eil.

2. al yo-vad___ goi e-chad, ha - me - ya - cha-dim,

ha - me - ya - cha-dim, shi - me - cha A - do - nai E.-lo-

hei - nu, A - do - nai_____ e - chad.

| | |
|---|---|
| Sho·meir, sho·meir Yis·ra·eil, | שׁוֹמֵר יִשְׂרָאֵל, |
| she·mor she·ei·rit Yis·ra·eil; | שְׁמוֹר שְׁאֵרִית יִשְׂרָאֵל, |
| Sho·meir, sho·meir Yis·ra·eil, | |
| she·mor she·ei·rit Yis·ra·eil. | |
| | |
| Ve·al yo·vad, ve·al yo·vad Yis·ra·eil, | וְאַל־יֹאבַד יִשְׂרָאֵל, |
| ve·al yo·vad, ve·al yo·vad Yis·ra·eil; | הָאוֹמְרִים שְׁמַע יִשְׂרָאֵל. |
| ha·o·me·rim, ha·o·me·rim, | |
| ha·o·me·rim She·ma Yis·ra·eil. | |
| | |
| Sho·meir, sho·meir goi e·chad, | שׁוֹמֵר גּוֹי אֶחָד, |
| she·mor she·ei·rit am e·chad; | שְׁמוֹר שְׁאֵרִית עַם אֶחָד, |
| Sho·meir, sho·meir goi e·chad, | |
| she·mor she·ei·rit am e·chad. | |
| | |
| Ve·al yo·vad, ve·al yo·vad goi e·chad, | וְאַל־יֹאבַד גּוֹי אֶחָד, |
| ve·al yo·vad, ve·al yo·vad goi e·chad; | הַמְיַחֲדִים שִׁמְךָ, |
| ha·me·ya·cha·dim, ha·me·ya·cha·dim | יְיָ אֱלֹהֵינוּ, |
|     shi·me·cha | |
| A·do·nai E·lo·hei·nu, A·do·nai e·chad. | יְיָ אֶחָד. |

Guardian of Israel, guard the remnant of Israel. Let not Israel perish, the
people that proclaims: Hear, O Israel. Guardian of a unique people, guard
the remnant of that people. Let them not perish, who proclaim You the
One God.

# (60)
# SHOSHANAT YAAKOV

Purim Piyyut

Folk Melody

Joyfully ( ♩ = 80)

Sho - sha - nat Ya - a - kov, tsa - ha - la - ve - sa - mei -
cha, bi - re - o - tam ya - chad, te - chei - let Mor - de -
chai. Sho - chei - let Mor - de - chai. Te - shu - a - tam ha - yi - ta la -
ne - tsach, ve - tik - va - tam be - chol dor__ va - dor. Le -
ho - di - a she - kol ko - ve - cha lo yei - vo - shu ve -
lo - yi - ka - le - mu la - ne tsach kol ha - cho - sim bach.___ A -
rur Ha - man a - sher bi - keish le - a - be - di
ba - ruch Mor - de - chai___ ha - ye - hu - di.___ Sho -

*D.C. al Fine*

82

Sho·sha·nat Ya·a·kov, tsa·ha·la
ve·sa·mei·cha,
bi·re·o·tam ya·chad, te·chei·let
Mor·de·chai.

שׁוֹשַׁנַּת יַעֲקֹב, צָהֲלָה וְשָׂמֵחָה,
בִּרְאוֹתָם יַחַד, תְּכֵלֶת מָרְדְּכַי.

Te·shu·a·tam ha·yi·ta la·ne·tsach,

ve·tik·va·tam be·chol dor va·dor.

תְּשׁוּעָתָם הָיִיתָ לָנֶצַח,
וְתִקְוָתָם בְּכָל דּוֹר וָדוֹר.

Le·ho·dia she·kol ko·ve·cha  lo
yei·vo·shu
ve·lo yi·ka·le·mu la·ne·tsach kol
ha·cho·sim bach.

לְהוֹדִיעַ שֶׁכָּל קוֶֹיךָ לֹא יֵבֹשׁוּ
וְלֹא יִכָּלְמוּ לָנֶצַח כָּל הַחוֹסִים בָּךְ.

A·rur Ha·man a·sher bi·keish
le·a·be·di,
ba·ruch Mor·de·chai ha·ye·hu·di.

אָרוּר הָמָן אֲשֶׁר בִּקֵּשׁ לְאַבְּדִי,
בָּרוּךְ מָרְדְּכַי הַיְּהוּדִי.

The Jews of Shushan shouted with joy when they all saw Mordechai robed
in purple. You have always been their deliverance, their hope in every gen-
eration: to show that those who rest their hope in You will never be shamed,
that those who trust in You will never be humiliated. Cursed is Haman,
who sought to make me perish; blessed is Mordechai the Jew!

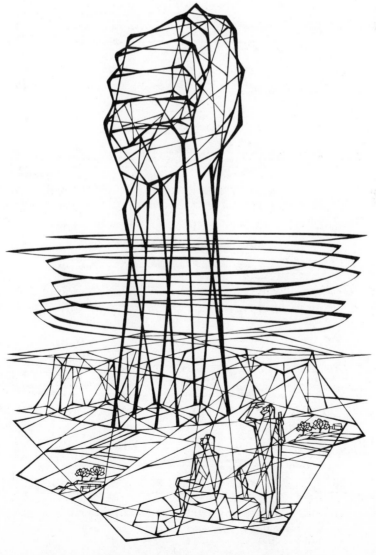

(p. 574)

# SONG OF THE PARTISANS

Adapted from the Hirsh Glik, Yiddish
English translation by Albert Friedlaender

Adapted from a melody by Pokras

March ( ♩ = 88)

You must not say that you now walk the fi - nal
*Zog nit kein mol az du geyst dem lets - tn*

way, be-cause the dark-ened heav-ens hide the blue of
*veg, ven him - len blai - e - ne far-shte - ln bloy - e*

day. The time we've longed for will at last draw
*teg. Vail ku - men vet noch und - zer oys - ge-benk - te*

near, And our___ steps, as drums, will sound that we are
*sho, S'vet a poyk ton und - zer trot: mir zen - en*

here. The time we've longed for will at last draw
*do! Vail ku - men vet noch und - zer oys - ge-benk - te*

near, And our___ steps, as drums, will sound that we are here.
*sho, S'vet a poyk ton und - zer trot: mir zen - en do!*

From land all green with palms to
    lands all white with snow,
We now arrive with all our pain
    and all our woe.
Where our blood sprayed out and
    came to touch the land,
There our courage and our faith
    will rise and stand.
    *(Repeat last 4 lines)*

Fun grinem palmen-land biz
    vaysin land fun shney,
Mir zainen do mit undzer pain
    mit undzer vey.
Un vu gefaln siz a shprits
    fun undzer blut,
Vet a shprotz ton undzer g'vure
    undzer mut.
    *(Repeat last 4 lines)*

(48)

# SPRING-TIDE OF THE YEAR

Alice Lucas

from *Union Haggadah* (1907)

Behold, it is the spring-tide of the year! Over and past is winter's gloomy reign. The happy time of singing birds is here, And clad in bud and bloom are hill and plain.

And in the spring, when all the earth and sky
Rejoice together, still from age to age
Rings out the solemn chant of days gone by,
Proclaiming Israel's sacred heritage.

For as from out the house of bondage went
The host of Israel, in their midst they bore

The heritage of law and freedom, blent
In holy unity for evermore.

And still from rising unto setting sun
Shall this our heritage and watchword be:
"The Lord our God, the Lord our God is One,
And law alone it is that makes us free!"

85

(p. 364 & No. 25)

# SWEET HYMNS AND SONGS
## (ANIM ZEMIROT)

Alice Lucas, from 13th C. Piyyut                                        Traditional Melody

Lyrically ( ♩ = 96)

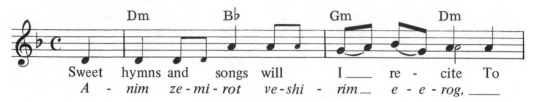

Sweet hymns and songs will I __ re - cite To
*A - nim ze - mi - rot ve - shi - rim __ e - e - rog, __*

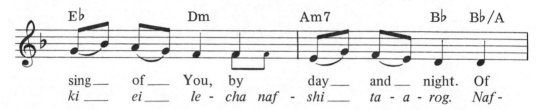

sing __ of __ You, by day __ and __ night. Of
*ki __ ei __ le - cha naf - shi __ ta - a - rog. Naf-*

You, who are my __ soul's __ de - light, Of
*shi chi - me - da be - tseil __ ya - de - cha la-*

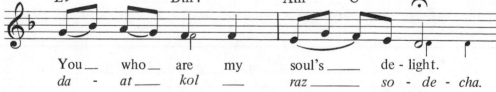

You __ who __ are my soul's __ de - light.
*da - at __ kol __ raz __ so - de - cha.*

How does my soul within me yearn
Beneath Your shadow to return,
Your secret mysteries to learn.

And e'en while yet Your glory fires
My words, and hymns of praise inspires,
Your love it is my heart desires.

My meditation day and night,
May it be pleasant in Your sight,
For You are all my soul's delight.

נַפְשִׁי חָמְדָה בְּצֵל יָדֶיךָ,
לָדַעַת כָּל־רָז סוֹדֶךָ.

מִדֵּי דַבְּרִי בִּכְבוֹדֶךָ,
הוֹמֶה לִבִּי אֶל־דּוֹדֶיךָ.

יֶעֱרַב־נָא שִׂיחִי עָלֶיךָ,
כִּי נַפְשִׁי תַעֲרוֹג אֵלֶיךָ.

86

## (54)
# TAKE UNTO YOU

Alice Lucas

Samuel Alman
Based on Sukkot melody

Stately (♩ = 80)

"Take un-to you the boughs__ of __ good-ly trees,

Branch-es of palm, and wil-lows of the brook.

*(Organ or humming—no chords)* And

build__ you booths in which to dwell with these."__

So it was writ-ten in the sa-cred book.

Thus kept they harvest in the years gone by,
And blessed the Lord for all His bounteous store,
And songs of praise and prayer arose on high
To Him whose mercies are for evermore.

Afield no longer as in ancient days
We go to gather corn and wine and oil;
Yet still, O Lord, we come with prayer and praise,
To seek Your blessing on our harvest toil.

For toilers in the field of life are we;
Whether amidst green meadows smooth and fair,
Or tracks of barren land our portion be,
You, Lord, have bidden us to labor there.

Hear, then, our prayer this day, and deign to bless
The precious seed we scatter far and wide,
That with rejoicing and with thankfulness,
We may bring home our sheaves at harvest-tide.

# (68)
# THE NATIONAL ANTHEM

Francis Scott Key

John Stafford Smith

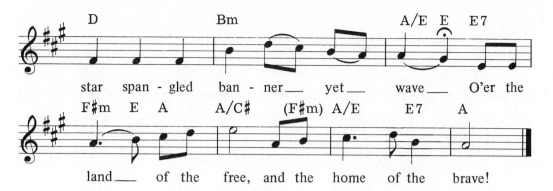

star span - gled ban - ner___ yet___ wave___ O'er the

land___ of the free, and the home of the brave!

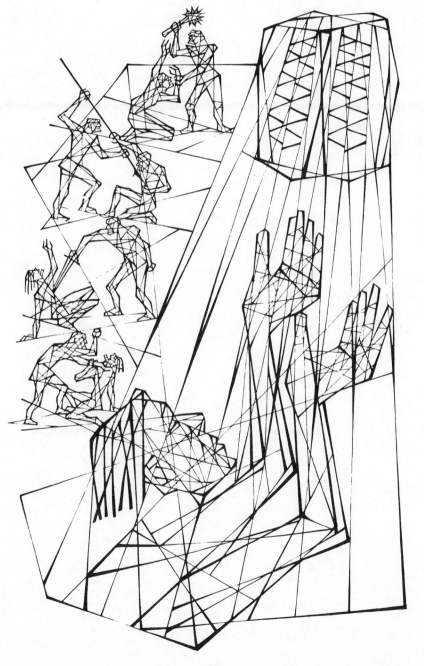

## (2 & 1)
# THE LORD OF ALL
### (Alternate Melody for Adon Olam)

Adapted from English
translation by Frederic DeSola Mendes

Herbert Fromm

**Majestically ( ♩ = 96)**

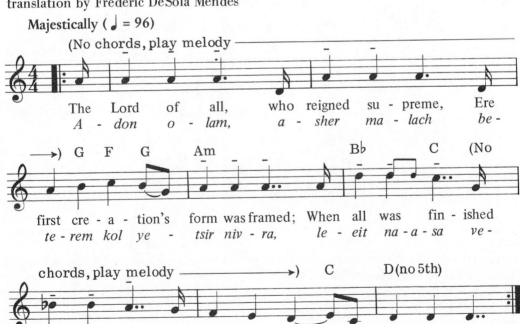

The Lord of all, who reigned su - preme, Ere
*A - don o - lam, a - sher ma - lach be -*

first cre - a - tion's form was framed; When all was fin - ished
*te - rem kol ye - tsir niv - ra, le - eit na - a - sa ve -*

by His will, His name Al - might - y was pro - claimed.
*chef - tso kol, a - zai me - lech__ she - mo nik - ra.*

# THERE LIVES A GOD'

James K. Guttheim
(Translated from the Hamburg Temple Hymnal)

Otto Lob

Resolutely ( ♩ = 92)

There lives a God! Each fi - nite crea - ture pro-claims His rule on sea and land; Through-out all chang - ing forms of na - ture is clear - ly shown His might - y hand. In ev - 'ry place is heard the call: "The Lord of Hosts has made us all."

There lives a God! Each finite creature
Proclaims His rule on sea and land;
Throughout all changing forms of nature
Is clearly shown His mighty hand.
In ev'ry place is heard the call:
"The Lord of Hosts has made us all."

Through nights of elemental strife.
Wherever God does choose my way,
I follow Him without dismay.

There lives a God! Though storms are sweeping
Across our pilgrim paths of life,
More bright the morn that ends the weeping

There is a God! When life is waning,
His love is near from dread to save;
My years are all of His ordaining
He only taketh what He gave.
The grave shall not end all for me,
Thou livest, God, I live in Thee.

# (24)
# TOV LEHODOT

Based on Psalm 92

Max Janowski

92

tov ___ le - ho - dot,  tov  le - ho - dot  la - do -

nai.  Le - ha - gid _____ ba -

bo - ker  chas - de -

cha  ve - e - mu - na - te - cha  ba -

lei - lot,  ba - lei - lot.

Tov, tov, tov le·ho·dot,
tov le·ho·dot la·a·do·nai.

U·le·za·meir le·shi·me·cha, El·yon,
le·shi·me·cha El·yon.

Tov, tov . . . .

Le·ha·gid ba·bo·ker chas·de·cha
ve·e·mu·na·te·cha ba·lei·lot.

Tov, tov . . . .

טוֹב, טוֹב, טוֹב לְהוֹדוֹת,
טוֹב לְהוֹדוֹת לַיָי.

וּלְזַמֵר לְשִׁמְךָ עֶלְיוֹן,
לְשִׁמְךָ עֶלְיוֹן.

טוֹב, טוֹב. . . .

לְהַגִיד בַּבֹּקֶר חַסְדֶּךָ
וֶאֱמוּנָתְךָ בַּלֵילוֹת.

טוֹב, טוֹב. . . .

It is good to give thanks to the Lord, to sing praises to Your name, O Most
High!

93

# (59)
# UTSU EITSA

Isaiah 8:10

Folk Melody

U·tsu ei·tsa ve·tu·far;
da·be·ru da·var ve·lo ya·kum:
ki i·ma·nu Eil.

עוּצוּ עֵצָה וְתֻפָר;
דַּבְּרוּ דָבָר וְלֹא יָקוּם:
כִּי עִמָּנוּ אֵל.

Make your plans — they will be annulled; scheme against us — it will not
avail — for God is with us.

# (19)

# VATIK

Piyyut                                                    Chaim Banet

Lyrically (♩ = 96)

cha.   Ei-leh cha-me - dah,   cha-me-dah li - bi,   ve-chu-sa

na   ve - al na tit - a - leim.   Ei-leh cha-me - dah,   cha-me-dah li -

bi   ve - chu - sa   na   ve - al   na tit - a - leim.

| | |
|---|---|
| Va·tik, ye·he·mu na ra·cha·me·cha, | וָתִיק, יֶהֱמוּ נָא רַחֲמֶיךָ, |
| ve·chu·sa na al bein a·hu·ve·cha. | וְחוּסָה נָא עַל בֵּן אֲהוּבֶךָ. |
| Ki zeh ka·ma nich·sof nich·saf·ti | כִּי זֶה כַּמָּה נִכְסוֹף נִכְסַפְתִּי |
| lir·ot be·tif·e·ret u·ze·cha. | לִרְאוֹת בְּתִפְאֶרֶת עֻזֶּךָ. |
| Ei·leh cha·me·da li·bi, | אֵלֶּה חָמְדָה לִבִּי, |
| ve·chu·sa na ve·al na tit·a·leim. | וְחוּסָה נָא וְאַל נָא תִּתְעַלֵּם. |

God our Reliance, let Your pity be stirred up for Your beloved child. I have yearned so long to see Your glorious might. This is my heart's desire; have pity: hide Yourself no more.

# VEHAEIR EINEINU

Liturgy

Shlomo Carlebach

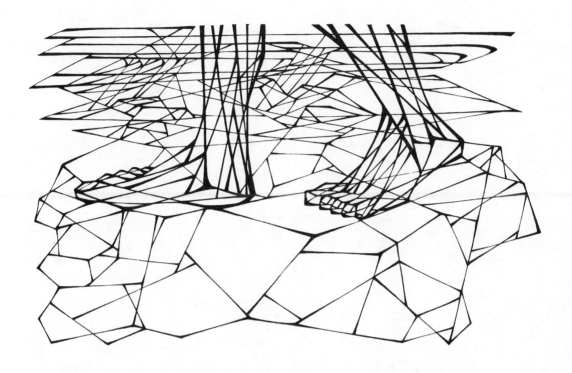

| | |
|---|---|
| Ve·ha·eir ei·nei·nu be·to·ra·te·cha, | וְהָאֵר עֵינֵינוּ בְּתוֹרָתֶךָ, |
| ve·da·beik li·bei·nu be·mits·vo·te·cha, | וְדַבֵּק לִבֵּנוּ בְּמִצְוֹתֶיךָ, |
| ve·ya·cheid le·va·vei·nu | וְיַחֵד לְבָבֵנוּ |
| le·a·ha·va u·le·yir·a et she·me·cha. | לְאַהֲבָה וּלְיִרְאָה אֶת־שְׁמֶךָ. |
| Ve·lo nei·vosh | וְלֹא נֵבוֹשׁ |
| ve·lo ni·ka·leim | וְלֹא נִכָּלֵם |
| ve·lo ni·ka·sheil | וְלֹא נִכָּשֵׁל |
| le·o·lam va·ed. | לְעוֹלָם וָעֶד. |

Enlighten our eyes in Your Torah, cause our hearts to cling to Your Mitzvot, and unite our hearts to love and revere Your name. Then we shall not be shamed, nor humiliated, nor shall we ever stumble.

99

# VEHEISHIV LEIV AVOT

Malachi 3:23-24

Chassidic Melody

Hi·nei a·no·chi sho·lei·ach la·chem

El·li·ya·hu ha·na·vi

li·fe·nei bo yom A·do·nai;

Ve·hei·shiv leiv a·vot al ba·nim

ve·leiv ba·nim al a·vo·tam.

הִנֵּה אָנֹכִי שֹׁלֵחַ לָכֶם

אֵלִיָּהוּ הַנָּבִיא

לִפְנֵי בּוֹא יוֹם יְיָ:

וְהֵשִׁיב לֵב אָבוֹת עַל בָּנִים

וְלֵב בָּנִים עַל אֲבוֹתָם.

Behold, I am sending to you Elijah the prophet, before the coming of the day of the Lord: and he will cause the hearts of the parents to turn to the children, and the hearts of the children to the parents.

# (22)
# VETAHEIR LIBEINU

Liturgy

Chassidic Melody

Ve·ta·heir li·bei·nu le·ov·de·cha be·e·met.

וְטַהֵר לִבֵּנוּ לְעָבְדְּךָ בֶּאֱמֶת. ▄

Purify our hearts to serve You in truth.

101

# YAH RIBON

Israel Najara, 16th C.

Chassidic Melody

Yah ri·bon a·lam ve·al·ma·ya,
ant Hu mal·ka, me·lech mal·cha·ya.
O·vad ge·vur·teich, ve·tim·ha·ya,
she·far ko·da·mai, le·ha·cha·va·ya.

Yah ri·bon . . .

יָהּ רִבּוֹן עָלַם וְעָלְמַיָּא,
אַנְתְּ הוּא מַלְכָּא, מֶלֶךְ מַלְכַיָּא.
עוֹבַד גְּבוּרְתֵּךְ, וְתִמְהַיָּא,
שְׁפַר קֳדָמַי לְהַחֲוָיָה.

יָהּ רִבּוֹן עָלַם וְעָלְמַיָּא,
אַנְתְּ הוּא מַלְכָּא מֶלֶךְ מַלְכַיָּא.

She·va·chin a·sa·deir, tsaf·ra
  ve·ram·sha,
lach, E·la·ha ka·di·sha, di ve·ra chol
  naf·sha.

I·rin ka·di·shin, u·ve·nei e·na·sha,
chei·vat ba·ra, ve·o·fei she·ma·ya.

Yah ri·bon . . .

שְׁבָחִין אֲסַדֵּר, צַפְרָא וְרַמְשָׁא,
לָךְ, אֱלָהָא קַדִּישָׁא דִּי בְרָא כָל־
נַפְשָׁא.
עִירִין קַדִּישִׁין, וּבְנֵי אֲנָשָׁא,
חֵיוַת בָּרָא, וְעוֹפֵי שְׁמַיָּא.
יָהּ רִבּוֹן עָלַם וְעָלְמַיָּא,
אַנְתְּ הוּא מַלְכָּא מֶלֶךְ מַלְכַיָּא.

Rav·re·vin o·ve·dach, ve·ta·ki·fin,
ma·cheich ra·ma·ya ve·za·keif ke·fi·fin,
Lu ye·chei ge·var she·nin a·le·fin,
la yei·ol ge·vur·teich be·chush·be·na·ya.

Yah ri·bon . . .

רַבְרְבִין עוֹבְדָיךְ, וְתַקִּיפִין,
מָכֵךְ רָמַיָּא וְזָקֵף כְּפִיפִין,
לוּ יִחֵא גְבַר שְׁנִין אַלְפִין,
לָא יֵעֹל גְּבוּרְתֵּךְ בְּחֻשְׁבְּנַיָּא.
יָהּ רִבּוֹן עָלַם וְעָלְמַיָּא,
אַנְתְּ הוּא מַלְכָּא מֶלֶךְ מַלְכַיָּא.

Lord God of this and all worlds, You are Supreme, the Sovereign
God. Your mighty, wondrous work moves my heart to praise You.

Evening and morning I praise You, Holy God who forms all beings:
angels and mortals, beasts and birds.

Great are Your works, and mighty; You humble the proud, and lift
up those who are bowed down. Were we to live a thousand years,
there would not be time enough to tell of Your might!

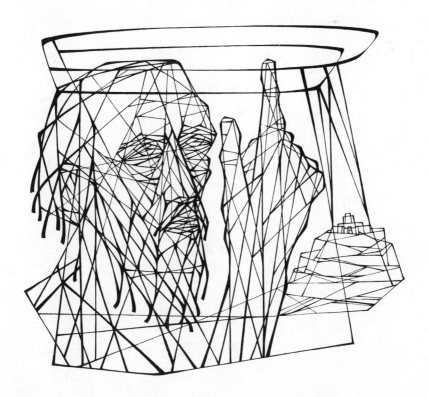

103

# (17)
# YEDID NEFESH

Piyyut

Ehud and Sara Zweig

la, la, la,) el mul ha - da - re - cha._____

Ye·did ne·fesh, av ha·ra·cha·man,
me·shoch av·de·cha el re·tso·ne·cha.
Ya·ruts av·de·cha ke·mo a·yal,
yish·ta·cha·veh el mul ha·da·re·cha.

יְדִיד נֶפֶשׁ, אָב הָרַחֲמָן,
מְשׁוֹךְ עַבְדְּךָ אֶל רְצוֹנֶךָ.
יָרוּץ עַבְדְּךָ כְּמוֹ אַיָּל,
יִשְׁתַּחֲוֶה אֶל מוּל הֲדָרֶךָ.

Heart's delight, Source of mercy, draw Your servant into Your arms: I leap
like a deer to stand in awe before You.

105

(pp. 592 & 611)

# YERUSHALAYIM

Avigdor Hameiri                                    Anonymous Melody

ru - sha - la - yim! mei - cho - re - vo - ta - yich ev - neich!____

ru - sha - la - yim! Ya - vo ha - me - shi - ach, ya - vo!____

ירושלים

מֵעַל פִּסְגַּת הַר הַצּוֹפִים, שָׁלוֹם לָךְ יְרוּשָׁלַיִם.

Mei·al pis·gat har ha·tso·fim, sha·lom lach Ye·ru·sha·la·yim.

מֵעַל פִּסְגַּת הַר הַצּוֹפִים, אֶשְׁתַּחֲוֶה לָךְ אַפָּיִם.

Mei·al pis·gat har ha·tso·fim, esh·ta·cha·veh lach a·pa·yim.

מֵעַל־פִּסְגַּת הַר הַצּוֹפִים, שָׁלוֹם לָךְ יְרוּשָׁלַיִם.

Mei·al pis·gat har ha·tso·fim, sha·lom lach Ye·ru·sha·la·yim.

אַלְפֵי גּוֹלִים מִקְצוֹת כָּל־תֵּבֵל, נוֹשְׂאִים אֵלַיִךְ עֵינַיִם.

A·le·fei go·lim mi·ke·tsot kol tei·veil, no·se·im ei·la·yich ei·na·yim.

בְּאַלְפֵי בְרָכוֹת הֱיִי בְרוּכָה, מִקְדַּשׁ מֶלֶךְ עִיר מְלוּכָה.

Be·a·le·fei ve·ra·chot ha·yi ve·ru·cha, mik·dash me·lech ir me·lu·cha:

יְרוּשָׁלַיִם, יְרוּשָׁלַיִם! אֲנִי לֹא אָזוּז מִפֹּה!

Ye·ru·sha·la·yim, Ye·ru·sha·la·yim! A·ni lo a·zuz mi·po.

יְרוּשָׁלַיִם, יְרוּשָׁלַיִם! יָבֹא הַמָּשִׁיחַ, יָבֹא!

Ye·ru·sha·la·yim, Ye·ru·sha·la·yim! Ya·vo ha·ma·shi·ach, ya·vo!

From the peak of Mt. Scopus, shalom, Jerusalem. A thousand exiles
from all the ends of earth lift up their eyes to you. Be blessed with
a thousand blessings, O royal shrine, city of kings. Jerusalem,
O Jerusalem! I will not budge from this place! Jerusalem! O Jerusalem! Let the redemption come, let it come!

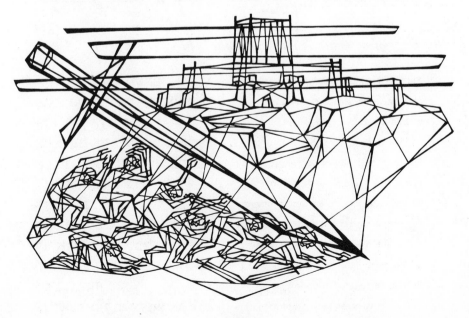

## (4 & 5)
# YIGDAL
### (We Praise the Living God)

Attributed to Daniel Ben Judah, 14th C.
English: composite

Myer Leoni

Majestically (♩ = 96)

| | Em | | Em7 | | Am | | Em | |
|---|---|---|---|---|---|---|---|---|
| Yig- | dal | E-lo-him chai | ve- | yish-ta- | bach, | nim- | | |
| *We* | *praise* | *the liv-ing God,* | *For-* | *ev-er praise His name,* | *who* | | | |

| | G/B | | Am7 | | G/B | | D7 | | G |
|---|---|---|---|---|---|---|---|---|---|
| tsa | ve-ein | eit | | el | me-tsi-u-to. | | | E- | |
| *was* | *and is* | *and* | *is* | *to* | *be for-e'er the same;* | *The* | | | |

| | Em | | Am/F# | | B | Em | | B |
|---|---|---|---|---|---|---|---|---|
| chad | ve-ein ya-chid | ke- | yi- | chu- | do, | ne- | | |
| *One* | *e-ter-nal God* | *be-* | *fore our world ap-pears,* | *And* | | | | |

| | Em | | C | | | Em/B B7 | Em |
|---|---|---|---|---|---|---|---|
| lam | ve-gam ein sof | | le- | ach-du-to. | | | |
| *there* | *can be* | *no* | *end* | *of time be-yond His years.* | | | |

| | |
|---|---|
| Yig-dal E-lo-him chai ve-yish-ta-bach, | יִגְדַּל אֱלֹהִים חַי וְיִשְׁתַּבַּח, |
| nim-tsa ve-ein eit el me-tsi-u-to. | נִמְצָא וְאֵין עֵת אֶל־מְצִיאוּתוֹ. |
| E-chad ve-ein ya-chid ke-yi-chu-do, | אֶחָד וְאֵין יָחִיד כְּיִחוּדוֹ, |
| ne-lam ve-gam ein sof le-ach-du-to. | נֶעְלָם וְגַם אֵין סוֹף לְאַחְדּוּתוֹ. |
| Ein lo de-mut ha-guf ve-ei-no guf, | אֵין לוֹ דְמוּת הַגּוּף וְאֵינוֹ גוּף, |
| lo na-a-roch ei-lav ke-du-sha-to. | לֹא נַעֲרוֹךְ אֵלָיו קְדֻשָׁתוֹ. |
| Kad-mon le-chol da-var a-sher niv-ra, | קַדְמוֹן לְכָל־דָּבָר אֲשֶׁר נִבְרָא, |
| ri-shon ve-ein rei-shit le-rei-shi-to. | רִאשׁוֹן וְאֵין רֵאשִׁית לְרֵאשִׁיתוֹ. |
| Hi-no a-don o-lam, le-chol no-tsar | הִנּוֹ אֲדוֹן עוֹלָם, לְכָל־נוֹצָר |
| yo-reh ge-du-la-to u-mal-chu-to. | יוֹרֶה גְדֻלָּתוֹ וּמַלְכוּתוֹ. |
| She-fa ne-vu-a-to ne-ta-no, | שֶׁפַע נְבוּאָתוֹ נְתָנוֹ, |
| el a-ne-shei se-gu-la-to ve-tif-ar-to. | אֶל־אַנְשֵׁי סְגֻלָּתוֹ וְתִפְאַרְתּוֹ. |

| | |
|---|---|
| Lo kam be·yis·ra·eil ke·mo·sheh od | לֹא קָם בְּיִשְׂרָאֵל כְּמשֶׁה עוֹד |
| na·vi u·ma·bit et te·mu·na·to, | נָבִיא וּמַבִּיט אֶת־תְּמוּנָתוֹ, |
| To·rat e·met na·tan le·a·mo Eil, | תּוֹרַת אֱמֶת נָתַן לְעַמּוֹ אֵל, |
| al yad ne·vi·o ne·e·man bei·to. | עַל יַד נְבִיאוֹ נֶאֱמַן בֵּיתוֹ. |
| Lo ya·cha·lif ha·eil, ve·lo ya·mir | לֹא יַחֲלִיף הָאֵל, וְלֹא יָמִיר |
| da·to, le·o·la·mim le·zu·la·to. | דָּתוֹ, לְעוֹלָמִים לְזוּלָתוֹ. |
| Tso·feh ve·yo·dei·a se·ta·rei·nu, | צוֹפֶה וְיוֹדֵעַ סְתָרֵינוּ, |
| ma·bit le·sof da·var be·kad·ma·to. | מַבִּיט לְסוֹף דָּבָר בְּקַדְמָתוֹ. |
| Go·meil le·ish che·sed ke·mif·a·lo, | גּוֹמֵל לְאִישׁ חֶסֶד כְּמִפְעָלוֹ, |
| no·tein le·ra·sha ra ke·rish·a·to. | נוֹתֵן לְרָשָׁע רַע כְּרִשְׁעָתוֹ. |
| Yish·lach le·keits ya·min pe·dut o·lam, | יִשְׁלַח לְקֵץ יָמִין פְּדוּת עוֹלָם, |
| kol chai ve·yeish ya·kir ye·shu·a·to. | כָּל־חַי וְיֵשׁ יַכִּיר יְשׁוּעָתוֹ. |
| Cha·yei o·lam na·ta be·to·chei·nu, | חַיֵּי עוֹלָם נָטַע בְּתוֹכֵנוּ, |
| ba·ruch a·dei ad sheim te·hi·la·to. | בָּרוּךְ עֲדֵי עַד שֵׁם תְּהִלָּתוֹ. |

Magnified and praised be the living God; His existence is eternal. He is One and unique in His unity; He is unfathomable, and His Oneness is unending. He has no bodily form, He is incorporeal; His holiness is beyond compare. He preceded all creation; He is the First, and He Himself has no beginning.

Behold the eternal Lord, who reveals His greatness and sovereignty to every creature. He inspired with the gift of prophecy those whom He chose to make known His glory.

Never has there been a prophet like Moses, whose closeness to God is unmatched. A Torah of truth did God give to His people, through His prophet, His faithful servant.

God does not change; His teaching will not be supplanted; He will always be the same. He watches us and knows our secret thoughts; He perceives the end of every matter before it begins.

He deals kindly with those who merit kindness, and brings upon the wicked the evil consequences of their deeds. At the end of days He will send an everlasting redemption; all that lives and breathes shall witness His deliverance.

He has implanted eternal life within us. Blessed is His glorious name to all eternity.

### YIGDAL (A Metrical Version)

We praise the living God,
For ever praise His name,
Who was and is and is to be
For e'er the same;

The One eternal God
Before our world appears,
And there can be no end of time
Beyond His years.

Without a form is He,
Nor can we comprehend
The measure of His love for us —
Without an end.

For He is Lord of all,
Creation speaks His praise.
The human race and all that grows
His will obeys.

He knows our every thought,
Our birth and death ordains;
He understands our fervent dreams,
Our hopes and our pains.
Eternal life has He
Implanted in our soul.
We dedicate our life to Him —
His way, our goal!

(p. 261)

# YISMECHU HASHAMAYIM

Psalm 96:11

Chassidic Melody

Yis · me · chu  ha · sha · ma · yim

ve · ta · geil  ha · a · rets.

Yir · am  ha · yam  u · me · lo · o.

יִשְׂמְחוּ הַשָּׁמַיִם
וְתָגֵל הָאָרֶץ.
יִרְעַם הַיָּם וּמְלֹאוֹ.

Let the heavens be glad and the earth rejoice. Let the sea roar
and all that fills it.

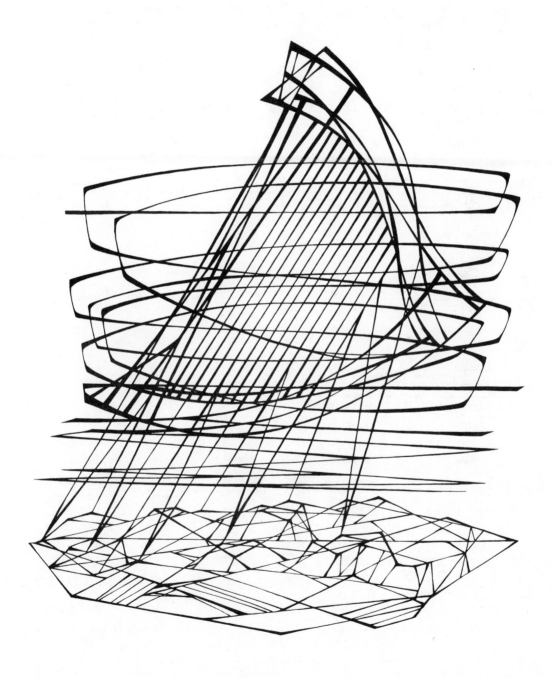

# (7)
# YOM ZEH LE-YISRA-EIL

Isaac Luria

Folk Melody

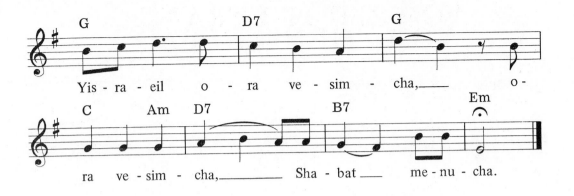

Yis-ra-eil    o - ra    ve - sim - cha,_____    o-

ra    ve - sim - cha,_____ Sha - bat ___ me - nu - cha.

Yom zeh le·yis·ra·eil o·ra ve·sim·cha,

Sha·bat me·nu·cha.

יוֹם זֶה לְיִשְׂרָאֵל אוֹרָה וְשִׂמְחָה,

שַׁבַּת מְנוּחָה.

Tsi·vi·ta pi·ku·dim be·ma·a·mad Si·nai,

Sha·bat u·mo·a·dim lish·mor be·chol
sha·nai,
la·a·roch le·fa·nai mas·eit va·a·ru·cha,

Sha·bat me·nu·cha.

צִוִּיתָ פִּקּוּדִים בְּמַעֲמַד סִינַי,

שַׁבָּת וּמוֹעֲדִים לִשְׁמוֹר בְּכָל־שָׁנַי,

לַעֲרוֹךְ לְפָנַי מַשְׂאֵת וַאֲרוּחָה,

שַׁבָּת מְנוּחָה.

Yom zeh le·yis·ra·eil o·ra ve·sim·cha,

Sha·bat me·nu·cha.

יוֹם זֶה לְיִשְׂרָאֵל אוֹרָה וְשִׂמְחָה,

שַׁבַּת מְנוּחָה.

Chem·dat ha·le·va·vot le·u·ma
she·vu·ra,
li·ne·fa·shot nich·a·vot ne·sha·ma
ye·tei·ra,
mi·ne·fesh me·tsei·ra ya·sir a·na·cha,

Sha·bat me·nu·cha.

חֶמְדַּת הַלְּבָבוֹת לְאֻמָּה שְׁבוּרָה,

לִנְפָשׁוֹת נִכְאָבוֹת נְשָׁמָה יְתֵרָה,

מִנֶּפֶשׁ מְצֵרָה יָסִיר אֲנָחָה,

שַׁבָּת מְנוּחָה.

Yom zeh le·yis·ra·eil o·ra ve·sim·cha,

Sha·bat me·nu·cha.

יוֹם זֶה לְיִשְׂרָאֵל אוֹרָה וְשִׂמְחָה,

שַׁבַּת מְנוּחָה.

Ki·dash·ta bei·rach·ta o·to mi·kol
ya·mim,
be·shei·shet ki·li·ta me·le·chet
o·la·mim,
bo ma·tse·u a·gu·mim hash·keit
u·vit·cha,
Sha·bat me·nu·cha.

קִדַּשְׁתָּ בֵּרַכְתָּ אוֹתוֹ מִכָּל־יָמִים,

בְּשֵׁשֶׁת כִּלִּיתָ מְלֶאכֶת עוֹלָמִים,

בּוֹ מָצְאוּ עֲגוּמִים הַשְׁקֵט וּבִטְחָה,

שַׁבָּת מְנוּחָה.

Yom zeh le·yis·ra·eil o·ra ve·sim·cha,

Sha·bat me·nu·cha.

יוֹם זֶה לְיִשְׂרָאֵל אוֹרָה וְשִׂמְחָה,

שַׁבַּת מְנוּחָה.

*This is Israel's day of light and joy, a Sabbath of rest.* You bade us, standing assembled at Sinai, that all the year through we should keep Your behest: To set out a table full-laden to honor the Sabbath of rest. *This is....*

Treasure of heart for the broken people, gift of new soul for the souls distressed, soother of sighs for the prisoned spirit: the Sabbath of rest. *This is....*

When the work of creating the world was done, You chose this day to be holy and blessed, that those heavy-laden find safety and stillness, a Sabbath of rest. *This is....*

# YOM ZEH MECHUBAD

Piyyut                                    Chassidic Melody

**Liltingly ( ♩ = 96 )**

Refrain:
Yom zeh me-chu-bad mi - kol ya - mim, mi - kol_ ya -
mim, ki vo sha-vat tsur o - la - mim, tsur o - la -
mim. Shei - shet ya - mim a - sei _ me-lach-te - cha, ve -
yom ha-she-vi - i lei - lo - he-cha, Sha-bat, Sha-bat lo
ta - a-seh vo me-la-cha, Ki chol a - sa _ shei-shet ya - mim.

| | |
|---|---|
| Yom zeh me·chu·bad ml·kol ya·mim, | יוֹם זֶה מְכֻבָּד מִכָּל־יָמִים, |
| ki vo sha·vat tsur o·la·mim. | כִּי בוֹ שָׁבַת צוּר עוֹלָמִים. |
| Shei·shet ya·mim a·sei me·lach·te·cha, | שֵׁשֶׁת יָמִים עֲשֵׂה מְלַאכְתֶּךָ, |
| ve·yom ha·she·vi·i lei·lo·he·cha, | וְיוֹם הַשְּׁבִיעִי לֵאלֹהֶיךָ, |
| Sha·bat lo ta·a·seh vo me·la·cha, | שַׁבָּת לֹא תַעֲשֶׂה בוֹ מְלָאכָה, |
| ki chol a·sa shei·shet ya·mim. | כִּי כֹל עָשָׂה שֵׁשֶׁת יָמִים. |
| Yom zeh ... | יוֹם זֶה. ... |
| Ha·sha·ma·yim me·sa·pe·rim ke·vo·do, | הַשָּׁמַיִם מְסַפְּרִים כְּבוֹדוֹ, |
| ve·gam ha·a·rets ma·le·a chas·do, | וְגַם הָאָרֶץ מָלְאָה חַסְדּוֹ, |
| re·u kol ei·leh a·se·ta ya·do, | רְאוּ כָּל־אֵלֶּה עָשְׂתָה יָדוֹ, |
| ki Hu ha·tsur po·o·lo ta·mim. | כִּי הוּא הַצּוּר פָּעֳלוֹ תָמִים. |
| Yom zeh ... | יוֹם זֶה. ... |

*This is the day most blessed of all, this is the day of the Creator's rest.* Six are your days of labor, the seventh devote to your God; on Shabbat refrain from work for gain: celebrate rather the work of creation. *This is the day . . . .* The heavens declare His glory, earth is full of His love; See it all — His handiwork, the Rock whose work is pure. *This is the day . . . .*

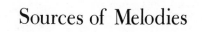

Sources of Melodies

# Sources of Melodies

The Joint Publication Committee of the American Conference of Cantors and the Central Conference of American Rabbis has made a conscientious effort to ascertain the copyright status of the melodies and texts used in this volume. We express our sincerest gratitude to all those mentioned below who have graciously granted permission as indicated. If no copyright markings are shown, it may be assumed that the work is in the public domain.

## ABBREVIATIONS OF SOURCES

CCAR — Central Conference of American Rabbis, 790 Madison Ave., New York, N. Y. 10021.

HUCBAS — Hebrew Union College Biblical and Archaeological School, Jerusalem. *Selections from the Sabbath and Holiday Services.* (The Sacred Music Press).

NJSB — *The New Jewish Song Book*, compiled and edited by Harry Coopersmith. (N. Y., Behrman House, Inc.) © Harry Coopersmith (deceased), 1965.

SMP — The Sacred Music Press of the Hebrew Union College - Jewish Institute of Religion, 40 West 68th Street, New York, N. Y. 10023.

SWS — *The Songs We Sing*, selected and edited by Harry Coopersmith. (N. Y., The United Synagogue Commission on Jewish Education, 1950). © The United Synagogue of America, 3080 Broadway, New York, N. Y. 10027.

SZ — *Songs of Zion*, compiled and edited by Harry Coopersmith. (N. Y., Behrman House, Inc., 1942) © Behrman's Jewish Book House, 1261 Broadway, New York, N. Y. 10018.

TCL — Transcontinental Music Publications, Union of American Hebrew Congregations, 838 Fifth Avenue, New York, N. Y. 10021.

UH — *Union Hymnal*. (N. Y., Central Conference of American Rabbis, 1933). vol. I — nos. 1–266; vol. II — nos. 267–341.

US — *Union Songster* (N. Y., Central Conference of American Rabbis, 1960).

## SPECIAL ACKNOWLEDGMENTS

We are grateful to all the publishers mentioned above for the use of selections in their publications. Gratitude is also extended to:

ACUM Ltd., P.O.B. 11201, Tel Aviv 61110, Israel. For: *Al Shelosha Devarim, David Melech, Eili Eili, Lecha Dodi, Ma Navu, Yedid Nefesh.*

SHLOMO CARLEBACH, 888 Seventh Ave., New York, N. Y. 10019. For: *Esa Einai, Vehaeir Eineinu.*

JUDITH K. EISENSTEIN, For: texts of In the Wilderness, Who Can Retell. (*Mi Yemaleil*).

MRS. MAX HELFMAN, 16-C Via Castilla, Laguna Hills, CA 92653. For her late husband's *Early Will I Seek You.*

DR. MAX JANOWSKI, 8252 Woodlawn Avenue, Chicago, IL 60619. For: *Tov Lehodot.*

RICHARD NEUMANN, Board of Jewish Education, 426 East 58th Street, New York, N. Y. 10019. For: *Israel in Song.*

VELVEL PASTERNAK, Tara Publications, 29 Derby Avenue, Cedarhurst, N. Y. 11516. For: *Israel in Song, Songs of the Chassidim.*

HEINRICH SCHALIT, Box 347, Evergreen, CO 80439. For: *Anim Zemirot.*

Sources marked * have arrangements with keyboard accompaniments.

| TITLE | COMPOSER | SOURCE |
|---|---|---|
| Adon Olam | Eliezer Gerovitch | *UH 276, *US 8 |
| (alternate) | Herbert Fromm | *Hymns and Songs for the Synagogue © SMP |
| Al Hanisim | | HJSB 34 |
| Al Shelosha Devarim | Chaim Zur | © Osnat Publishing Co., Ltd., Israel |
| All the World | A. W. Binder | *UH 63, *US 32 © CCAR |
| Amar Rabbi Akiva | | |
| Amar Rabbi Elazar | | Silbermintz, Songs of Israel |
| America the Beautiful | Samuel Augustus Ward | *UH 262, *US 360 |
| Ani Maamin | | *SWS 374 |
| Anim Zemirot | Heinrich Schalit | *his Sabbath Morning Liturgy © Heinrich Schalit |
| Ashreinu | Shpirvarg | |
| Ata Echad | | SZ 150 |
| Baruch Eloheinu | | *SWS 217 |
| Come, O Holy Sabbath Evening | Pinchos Jassinowsky | *UH 105 © CCAR |
| Come, O Sabbath Day | A. W. Binder | *UH 118, *US 115 © CCAR |
| Could We With Ink | | *US 228 |
| David Melech | Mordecai Zeira | NJSB 162 © Tarbut Vechinuch, Israel |
| Deror Yikra | | HUCBAS 1 |
| Early Will I Seek You | Max Helfman | *SWS 395 © Mrs. Max Helfman |
| Eileh Chameda Libi | | Israel in Song, 56 |
| Eili Eili | David Zahavi | © Hamerkaz Letarbut Vechinuch, Israel |
| Ein Adir | | Israel in Song, 48 |
| Ein Keiloheinu | Julius Freudenthal | *UH 292 |
| (alternate) | Boruch Karliner | SWS 72 (with variations) |
| Esa Einai | Shlomo Carlebach | © Shlomo Carlebach |
| Father, Hear the Prayer | | NJSB 56 |
| From Heaven's Heights the Thunder Peals | | *UH 142 |
| God of Might | | *UH 207 |
| God of Our People | George W. Warren | *UH 263 |
| Halleluhu, Praise Him | | *US 204 |
| Hatikva | | Jewish Agency |
| Hoshia Et Amecha | | Songs of the Chassidim, #4 |
| How Good It Is | Louis Lewandowski | *UH 110, *US 112 |
| If Our God Had Not Befriended | Jacob Weinberg | *UH 123 |
| Im Ein Ani Li Mi Li? | | *US 44 |
| In the Wilderness | | *US 226 |
| Ivedu | | Songs of the Chassidim, #2 |
| Ki Eshmera Shabbat | | HUCBAS, 42 © SMP |
| Lecha Dodi | Louis Lewandowski | *UH 267, *US 112 |

| TITLE | COMPOSER | SOURCE |
|---|---|---|
| (alternate) | Mordecai Zeira | © Tarbut Vechinuch, Israel |
| Lo Yisa Goi | | *Israel in Song*, 44 |
| Magein Avot | Israel and Samuel E. Goldfarb | *Jewish Songster*, 161 |
| Ma Navu | Josef Spivak | © Edition Negen |
| Maoz Tsur | Benedetto Marcello | Eric Werner |
| (alternate) | | *SWS 129 |
| Menucha Vesimcha | | *SWS 30 |
| Mi Haish | | *Songs of the Chassidim*, #22 |
| Mi Yemaleil | Menashe Ravina | *US 260 |
| O God, Our Help | William Croft | *UH 47 |
| O Lord, Where Shall I | | |
| Find You? | Jacob Weinberg | *UH 21 |
| O Worship the King | Franz Josef Haydn | *UH 60, *US 35 |
| Pitechu Li | Jacob Beimel | *US 2 |
| Queen Sabbath | Pinchos Minkowsky | *US 116 |
| Rad Halaila | | NJSB 136 |
| Rock of Ages | | *UH 207 |
| Sachaki, Sachaki | | *SWS 376 |
| Shachar Avakeschecha | Isadore Freed | *Hassidic Service*, 7 © TCL |
| Shalom Aleichem | Israel Goldfarb | *UH 278, *US 118 |
| Shomeir Yisraeil | Israel Goldfarb | *Song and Praise for Sabbath Eve*, 114 |
| Shoshanat Yaakov | | *SWS 171 |
| Song of the Partisans | Pokras | *Our Musical Heritage*, 121 |
| Spring-Tide of the Year | | *UH 129 |
| Sweet Hymns and Songs | | *Hymns and Songs for the Synagogue* © SMP |
| Take Unto You | Samuel Alman | *UH 187, *US 426 © CCAR |
| The Lord of All | Herbert Fromm | *Hymns and Songs for the Synagogue* © SMP |
| The National Anthem | John Stafford Smith | *UH 265, *US 363 |
| There Lives A God | Otto Lob | *US 61 |
| Tov Lehodot | Max Janowski | *US 327 |
| Utsu Eitsa | | *US 252 |
| Vatik | Chaim Banet | |
| Vehaeir Eineinu | Shlomo Carlebach | *Israel in Song*, 46 © Shlomo Carlebach |
| Veheishiv Leiv Avot | | |
| Vetaheir Libeinu | | *US 42 |
| We Praise the Living God | Myer Leoni | *UH 277 |
| When This Song of Praise | | *US 22 |
| Yah Ribon | | |
| Yedid Nefesh | Ehud and Sara Zweig | © Osnat Publishing Co., Ltd., Israel |
| Yerushalayim | | *SWS 275 |
| Yigdal | Myer Leoni | *UH 277, *US 339 |
| Yismechu Hashamayim | | *Israel in Song*, 42 |
| Yom Zeh Leyisraeil | | *SWS 17 |
| Yom Zeh Mechubad | | *Songs of the Chassidim*, #54 |